SO-AAZ-485

Carolyn Lee Simmons
Oct 24 2006
74-77
Finished on
Halloween 10-31-06
at "Nell" while passing
out candy to
Trick & Treaters

Making JUDGMENTS Without Being JUDGMENTAL

Nurturing a Clear Mind
and a Generous Heart

TERRY D. COOPER

IVP Books

An imprint of InterVarsity Press
Downers Grove, Illinois

InterVarsity Press
P.O. Box 1400, Downers Grove, IL 60515-1426
World Wide Web: www.ivpress.com
E-mail: mail@ivpress.com

©2006 by Terry D. Cooper

All rights reserved. No part of this book may be reproduced in any form without written permission from InterVarsity Press.

InterVarsity Press® is the book-publishing division of InterVarsity Christian Fellowship/USA®, a student movement active on campus at hundreds of universities, colleges and schools of nursing in the United States of America, and a member movement of the International Fellowship of Evangelical Students. For information about local and regional activities, write Public Relations Dept., InterVarsity Christian Fellowship/USA, 6400 Schroeder Rd., P.O. Box 7895, Madison, WI 53707-7895, or visit the IVCF website at <www.intervarsity.org>.

All Scripture quotations, unless otherwise indicated, are taken from the Holy Bible, New International Version®. NIV®. Copyright ©1973, 1978, 1984 by International Bible Society. Used by permission of Zondervan Publishing House. All rights reserved.

Design: Cindy Kiple
Images: Todd Gispstein/Getty Images

ISBN-10: 0-8308-3323-4
ISBN-13: 978-0-8308-3323-8

Printed in the United States of America ∞

Library of Congress Cataloging-in-Publication Data

Cooper, Terry D.
    Making Judgments without being judgmental: nurturing a clear
mind and a generous heart/Terry D. Cooper.
        p. cm.
    Includes bibliographical references and indexes.
    ISBN-13: 978-0-8308-3323-8 (pbk.: alk. paper)
    ISBN-10: 0-8308-3323-8 (pbk.: alk. paper)
    1. Judgment—Religious aspects—Christianity. I. Title.
BV4597.54.C67 2006
241—dc22
                                    2006020861

| P | 19 | 18 | 17 | 16 | 15 | 14 | 13 | 12 | 11 | 10 | 9 | 8 | 7 | 6 | 5 | 4 | 3 | 2 | 1 |
| Y | 21 | 20 | 19 | 18 | 17 | 16 | 15 | 14 | 13 | 12 | 11 | 10 | 09 | 08 | 07 | 06 |

For

Stella Cooper,

Wanda Webb-Hilliard

and

Genevieve Landrum,

with love

and fond memories.

CONTENTS

ACKNOWLEDGMENTS

I want to thank some wonderful conversation partners and friends for their direct and indirect input into this book. Robert Asa has offered many suggestions, which I have used throughout the book. His helpful insights are deeply appreciated. David Johnson and Harrison "Bud" Peyton have also been very influential in the writing of these pages. And I would like to thank Dan Reynolds and Steve May for interesting and provocative conversations concerning religion, psychotherapy and culture.

I would like to thank Gary Deddo, a fine writer and scholar in his own right, for editorial help with this entire process. Gary's encouragement and careful attention to this project has modeled the combination of a clear mind and a generous heart.

As always, my family is an important source of support for all my efforts. My wife, Linda, works hard to help middle school students become less judgmental and more understanding of each other. My parents, Don and Barbara Cooper, offer warm and consistent encouragement. And my stepdaughters, Lori and Michelle, make life much richer through their humor and care.

And finally, I wish to dedicate this book to three women I miss very much: Stella Cooper, Wanda Webb-Hilliard and Genevieve Landrum. The first two were my grandmothers, and the third was a great-aunt who was as close to me as a grandmother. I want to honor their love, affection and acceptance, for which I have been greatly blessed. They loved deeply. It is with much gratitude that I dedicate this book to them.

1

I'M JUDGMENTAL, YOU'RE JUDGMENTAL

I remember walking into a hospital a few years ago and seeing a young girl sitting on a curb in front of the emergency room. She could not possibly have been over ten years old. She was petting a cat who seemed to greatly enjoy her company. I walked by the young girl and said, "Is that your cat?"

"No," she replied.

"I wonder how old it is?" I said.

"I don't know," she replied.

I then added, "I wonder if it is a boy or girl cat?"

"I don't know," she said, as she continued to pet the cat.

Then I asked, "I wonder if it is from a neighborhood around here?"

Looking at me somewhat annoyed she said, "I don't know. Is that *important* to you?"

I walked into the hospital with a smile on my face and a lesson learned. I was trying to place this cat in some sort of preconceived category: gender, age, "socio-economic status" and so on. I was seeking a label or category in which to place this cat. For this little girl, however, there was no need for all this classification and pigeonholing of the cat. In fact, my questions were rather distracting. What was important to her was that this was a cat who wanted to be petted, and she was a little girl who wanted to pet the cat. All the other factors, all of my categorical schemes, were missing the whole point of the experience. By forcing the cat into one of my mental categories, I was neglecting her simple desire to "encounter" the cat.

I have thought of this little girl often and doubt that she will ever know how much she helped me that day. It was a reminder of the many ways that we as human beings dull our experience and reduce our adventures in life by trying to fit everything into neat little categories. How often we have our labels in hand, our categories in mind and our stereotypes with us when we approach new people or situations. It often makes me feel safe and secure when I can put people in a proper category. It reduces my anxiety. Labeling them reduces the intensity of the encounter and helps me quickly know what to do with the differences between us.

While I don't like admitting it, differences can often frighten me a bit. Differences between myself and another can easily provoke anxiety, which is quickly perceived as a threat. This threat can push me into a dualistic, black-or-white way of thinking in which one of us is "right" and the other is not. Sometimes I'm quite capable of judging other people in a very unfair manner, placing them into a category that makes life more manageable for me. "Of course Joe thinks that way. . . . He's a fundamentalist." Or, "Of course Sally thinks that way. . . . She's a soft-headed liberal." These easy categories keep me from genuinely hearing and conversing with others. If I let my anxiety get the best of me, I often fall prey to defensive, self-protective mental habits. It's much easier to live in my own mental backyard.

Yet another possibility is equally real. I may hear a differing opinion and immediately start judging *myself* rather than someone else: *Jim seems to know what he's talking about, so I must really be stupid.* I may quickly withdraw my opinion and see the disagreement as just one more sign of how uninformed I am. If I keep bumping into highly opinionated people (and there are certainly a lot of them), my self-doubts and self-judgments may convince me that I have no right to voice an opinion at all: *I'll just listen to others; I'm not smart enough to offer anything to the conversation.*

An unfortunate aspect of life is that often the people who most need to question themselves *don't,* the people who most need to doubt their opinions *don't,* and the people who most need to respect the boundaries of others will intrusively invade and force their opinions whether we want them or not.

I know a couple whom I'll call Ken and Brenda. These two have a very difficult time communicating. Often Brenda is very confused and concerned that there is a great deal about herself that remains hidden from her. She easily doubts herself and wonders where her blinders are. After a disagreement, she usually asks herself, *Was I being unfair? Are there things about Ken's perspective I'm not seeing? What if I don't see myself accurately at all?* Brenda is blessed (or cursed) with conscientiousness about her own behavior and recognition that she needs other people's perspectives to see the world more accurately.

Her husband, Ken, who is often quite opinionated, is not troubled by self-inventory and certainly does not engage in self-recrimination. He often says to people, "I know what I want, and I say what I mean." Ken takes a great deal of pride in the fact that he "calls it the way it is." He *knows* reality when he bumps into it, and he is not encumbered by what he calls "Brenda's insecure mind."

Brenda is at a tremendous disadvantage in this relationship. The irony of it is that her disadvantage results from strength—the ability to see several angles on things. Ken is clear, direct and non-self-doubting. Part of the reason that things seem so *obvious* to him is that he has never bothered to take on other perspectives. He has the "inside truth" on things. So, when Brenda stops to hear his perspective and begins to doubt herself, he exploits that hesitation and sees it as "weakness." Ken can be extremely manipulative and push Brenda into even more self-doubts. His pushiness grows out of his narrow focus. He is locked into his perspective and entrenched so deeply that he appears to Brenda as strong in his convictions, while she is uncertain. The truth is that while Brenda has a much fuller grasp of the world and is tentative because she is comprehensive, Ken's tunnel vision gives him an emotional edge in the discussion. There are disadvantages to being open-minded!

JUST WHEN WE THINK WE'RE NOT JUDGMENTAL . . .

For quite some time, I have been interested in exploring the topic of judgmentalism . . . as long as it dealt with *other people's* judgmental tendencies. I've been quick to spot in other people the rigid, authoritarian attitudes and statements that I often don't like very much. I've engaged in a reactionary protest against their judgmental thinking. I have attacked all the stereotyping, labeling, pigeonholing and smug sense of certainty that went along with their rigid mentality. The black or white, simplistic reduction of complex issues seemed inhumane and unsatisfactory. How proud I was to point this out! What I did not realize, of course, is that I was stuck in my own judgmentalism. By constantly reacting to others' judgmentalism, judgmentalism was actually controlling me. Yet I continued to throw stones at the judgmental stone-throwers.

What I also did not realize was that my harsh condemnation of judgmental people was every bit as judgmental as anything *they* were saying. I was becoming a narrow-minded defender of open-mindedness. I was intolerant of intolerance. I was a zealous missionary who grandiosely thought it was my job to expand people's thinking. I was going to "control" those awful controlling tendencies in other people. While the content of what I was saying may have differed from the judgmental attitudes I had encountered, the process of my thinking was the same.

I can remember spending hours talking to friends about how people were trying to "control" me: *How dare they do that! Who gave them the right to get into my business! They were disrespecting my ability to regulate my own life as they invaded my world with their narrow-minded thinking.* Yet what gradually began to dawn on me was that I was spending way too much time reacting to these reactionary people. I resented the fact that they did not accept me as I was. I didn't like their attempts to force their own opinions on me. Yet what became painfully clear is that I was equally trying to control them. I was not accepting them. I was demanding that they see life from my "open-minded" position. I was judging them for their judgmentalism. They wanted me to be different from who I was; yet I, too, wanted them to be different from who they really were.

I began to realize that judgmentalism and authoritarian thinking can come in many clothes. Again, I had recognized it only in perspectives I didn't like. Now I had to put my own style or manner of thinking under a microscope. I began to realize that a judgmental mentality can pop up in practically every area of life. In fact, many of us who pride ourselves on having transcended the narrow confines of rigid thinking are actually stuck in thought patterns that are very inflexible. Again, it is easy to become self-righteous precisely when we are pointing out the self-righteousness of others. *I'm so thankful,* I have unconsciously said to myself, *that I don't engage in those "primitive" thought patterns.*

My point is simply this: When we think we have completely eliminated judgmentalism from our thinking, we probably need to take another look. In fact, when we think we have "arrived" at a non-biased, completely neutral and totally fair-minded perspective, we're probably very deluded. Judgmental, authoritarian thinking is insidious, often sliding into our thoughts during times of anxiety and insecurity. It is not just "the other person's problem." In fact, I suspect it is *everyone's* predicament, at least to some degree. We can certainly make steps toward recognizing and changing it within ourselves, yet we will most likely never be completely free of it.

This brings us to a very important realization: The world is not simply divided between judgmental and nonjudgmental people. Everyone is judgmental in some ways and nonjudgmental in others. This is not an either/or issue. James Davison Hunter has effectively demonstrated that judgmental extremism occurs in both the right and left camps.[1] Therefore, we need to approach this topic with humility, compassion and awareness that unwarranted pride may have entered our own way of thinking.

One of my students recently gave me an interesting example of "open-minded" hypocrisy and reminded me that judgmentalism can show up in many different contexts. She attends a very liberal church where there is enormous focus on appreciating diversity and hearing everyone's perspective. The church clearly sees itself, she said, as different from more conservative churches because they welcome open dialogue. She told me that she would like to invite one of her friends to church, but her friend is pro-life. She went on to say that her Sunday morning class had been talking about social issues, and it became very clear to her that if anyone was not pro-choice, they would be "raked over the coals." The issue was so clear-cut that there could not possibly be an argument coming from the other side. She went on to say, "I'm pro-choice myself, but my class cannot see any legitimacy in any pro-life perspective. I would literally be afraid of what might be said to my friend." She added, "My friend is a wonderful person with a deep commitment to pro-life, and she has really thought through these issues." Yet given the mindset of the group, she was afraid for her friend to attend.

Another example of judgmental thinking can be seen in the extremist reactions to Mel Gibson's movie *The Passion of the Christ*. Some judgmental people on the right wanted to denounce anyone who thought the film had antisemitic tones or was too violent. Yet, in this case, I saw far more judgmentalism on the left. Time and again, Gibson's motives for doing this film were reduced to his desire to get rich, his pathologically violent tendencies and his desire to depict a macho Jesus. Gibson's own testimony of being deeply moved to make the film was cynically downplayed. There was such a strong protest against the film in some circles that it bordered on prohibition. Many of these same "open-minded" filmgoers had been very critical of the conservative protest of Martin Scorsese's film *The Last Temptation of Christ* several years earlier. Conservatives, they said, were condemning a film they had never seen. Yet were not "liberals" doing the same thing: making loud pronouncements on a film they didn't bother to watch? One of my friends, after scowling at me when she found out that I had attended the film, asked me, in a rather hostile manner, to explain myself.

My point here is not to stir up further controversy about this film but to point out some of the judgmentalism in those of us who think we have far surpassed any narrow-minded leanings. As I have pointed out, rigidity of thought can show up in *both* conservative and liberal climates. While the word *liberal* has sometimes meant generous or open to alternative opinions, a tense ideology can easily set in, a framework that becomes just as defensive as any form of conservative fundamentalism. Diversity is welcomed as long as the diversity is in agreement with the prevailing ideology. The moment that ideology is challenged, however, many "liberals" react with hostile defensiveness. They become dogmatically opposed to dogmatism, fanatical about fanaticism, intolerant of intolerance and rigid about rigidity.

Again, if we are to sincerely seek greater dialogue, we must look behind our easy self-congratulations that we are champions of open-mindedness, guardians of free inquiry and open to all perspectives. We, too, can villainize an opposing viewpoint, castigate the person behind the argument and demonstrate a severe insensitivity toward those with whom we disagree.

Indeed, judgmental people (which at one time or another includes each of us) are often very difficult. Yet if we extend to them the very judgments we so often receive from them, we perpetuate a cycle of intolerance that can lead to hatred. When we hear sarcastic, unfair comments, our knee-jerk tendency is to respond in like manner. Reactivity begets reactivity. It's hard to keep our balance when we've been clobbered by judgmentalism.

It is doubtful that any of us really believe we are closed-minded. We want to see ourselves as being fair. It is important, therefore, to drop our guard long enough to examine carefully our own dispositions. Again, our anger and protests against other viewpoints can cloud our rationality as we pontificate from our emotional reactions. While we may strain to be cordial, our private conversations include all-or-nothing expletives to describe a "stupid" idea or "crazy" person. Even in colleges and universities, where flexible thinking and open-mindedness are presented as ideals, there is often a stubborn resistance and dogmatic campaign against other perspectives. Lip service may be given to a respect for diversity, but there is often tremendous infighting and put-downs of people with alternative beliefs. At times, it is very difficult to find a balance in discussions where a variety of opinions are presented. Many years of schooling hardly guarantees that our opinion will be less judgmental, our reaction less extreme or our intolerance minimized. Many of us could name specific professors in universities who will not even speak to each other because of entrenched disagreements about theoretical points. They will not grant even the slightest legitimacy to others' viewpoints, yet they head toward their classes and talk about the importance of diversity in education.

I've also known counselors or psychotherapists who talk about tolerance for ambiguity with their clients, stress the significance of perspective-taking skills in counseling, then turn right around and argue passionately in a staff meeting that their style of therapy is the only legitimate one in mental health! What happened to the perspective-taking skills they valued a few minutes ago? What happened to their tolerance for ambiguity?

DEALING WITH JUDGMENTALISM

The first step in dealing effectively with judgmentalism is fully recognizing how slippery, conniving and insidious it can be. We may become *less* judgmental, but it is doubtful that we'll ever be completely *nonjudgmental*. Therefore, humility is needed.

My suggestion, as we explore the topic of judgmentalism, is to begin with the assumption that we *are* judgmental. Let's move away from an "us" and "them" mentality that focuses on the judgmentalism out there. Nonjudgmentalism is much like humility—once you assume you have it, this is a pretty sure indicator that you don't.

Judgmentalism involves two forms of superiority. First is moral superiority. This is one of the primary reasons that Jesus tells us in Matthew 7:1 to "judge not." As we judge another person, we are acting as a condescending spectator, not as a player. We are pushing aside our own shortcomings, faults, limits and finitude while we assess another. But once we get off the bleachers and into the game, we may find that life is much more complex than our spectator position had realized. Second, judgmentalism also involves a deep sense of intellectual superiority insofar as we believe we are capable of evaluating the entire context of another's life, with all its variables. It is an arrogant illusion that we can size up someone's entire life; we simply don't know the whole story. We don't know how others have been hurt, the struggles of their lives or the overall context out of which they have lived. Some may think this sounds dangerously close to excusing another's behavior, but this is not at all what I am suggesting. I am simply saying that we, coming out of our own set of assumptions, viewpoints, limitations and cognitive finitude, cannot possibly deliver a "final verdict" about another's entire life. We may have very definite judgments about specific *acts* this person has committed, but we don't have the intellectual resources to determine the nature of his or her entire existence.

Perhaps one of the reasons Jesus warned so vigorously against judgmentalism is that it makes a god or idol of our own viewpoint. Judgmentalism always means forgetting our limitations and finitude; we think we've found a "place" from which to give a final estimate of another.

Perhaps you've had an experience similar to my own. On occasion, I've had an opportunity to really get to know someone whose life has involved some destructive behavior. A person I'll call Jill very deeply confided in me about the course her life had taken. She told me many things about her childhood, most of which were very difficult for her to say. Jill had been sexually abused by her uncle and virtually ignored by her parents. She spent most of the time with her rather detached grandparents. She developed negative views of herself, which she tried to hide behind a tough exterior. She developed a sense of belonging with a group of teenagers who were doing some destructive things. She eventually got in trouble with the law.

I'm not excusing Jill's behavior, but a person deeply hungry for love, acceptance and affirmation lived beneath Jill's skin. I *knew* this about her. She was capable of enormous kindness and fondness for others, especially unfortunate children, which is why it was difficult to be in a conversation with "upright" people when Jill's name was brought up. "That girl is a tramp," said one person. "She'll never amount to anything." The group then bemoaned a world full of Jills and condescendingly insinuated that they were very happy that their lives had never sunk to that level.

So there I was, boiling inside because I knew a different Jill. I did not say anything because Jill had confided in me personally. So I listened to a group of completely uninformed people who knew nothing about Jill's personal life tell me all about her. The whole time I thought, *I'd like to see how you would handle what she has been through.* All I said was, "Well, folks, we don't know the whole story."

Judgmentalism makes us more and more alienated from our own dark side. When we are shocked and preoccupied with the "horrible" actions of others, our attention is removed from our own destructive behavior. Focused on the deplorable behavior of outsiders, we are freed from looking at ourselves. In fact, we can tell ourselves that their behavior is unthinkable or unimaginable. We could never do something like that!

Harsh condemnations of others indicate a lack of grace and tender acceptance in our own lives. With so many things being unacceptable, we are afraid to shine the flashlight into our own closets. Consequently, we remain ignorant of our own hidden aspirations, unconscious motivations and capability for destructive behavior. We are simply afraid to explore ourselves. Why? Because we don't want those judgmental guns pointed at us. We don't have enough grace and acceptance to freely make that inward journey. The fear of condemnation is much greater than the assurance of acceptance.

In many ways, John 8:1-11 conveys all the ingredients we need for a comprehensive understanding of judgmentalism. A woman caught in the act of adultery was thrown down before Jesus as onlookers prepared to stone her to death. One may immediately wonder where the male in this story was and why he wasn't held to the same level of accountability as the woman. Nevertheless, the accusers maintained that according to the law of Moses, the woman should be stoned to death. Jesus, writing in the sand, suggested that whoever among them was without sin could cast the first stone. After each of them dropped their rocks and walked away, Jesus told the woman that he did not condemn her either. He told her to go and sin no more.

This scene tells us a great deal about the nature and dynamics of judgmentalism. First, the accusers were able to use the woman's sin as a method of self-avoidance. In other words, as long as they could focus on the external behavior of someone else, they did not have to look at their own sin. She served as an important distraction. Further, there was a complete identification of this woman's particular behavior with her entire personhood. She was "nothing but" an adulterer. Her humanity was not seen. Fixation on a single act blinded the accusers to the greater context of her life. No one asked about her life circumstances or her own particular struggles. No one dared empathize with this woman's plight.

While this may not have excused her behavior, it would have helped the onlookers see the greater context of her life and become more understanding. As a public accusation, this event was devastatingly shameful to the woman. Jesus, perhaps by drawing in the sand and not making eye contact with the woman, refused to bring her further shame. Jesus also encouraged the accusers to turn their attention back toward their own lives. He would not allow them to scapegoat this woman. And when the accusers had left, Jesus approached the woman with kindness, which did not overlook an important ethical principle. The woman was not told that her behavior was exonerated, overlooked or no big deal; instead, she was encouraged to change her life. This was not cheap grace, an acceptance that did not invite repentance. Jesus honored the woman and essentially said that she had too much value and dignity to live as she had been living.

Judgmentalism, on the other hand, enhances self-righteousness through putting others down. One of the biggest psychological payoffs of judgmentalism is feeling proud that we are not like "those other people." We are one-up on them. Temporarily forgetting our own humanity, we are entitled to evaluate another human being. In fact, it's very easy to fall in love with the job of measuring and ranking others.

We may not consciously be aware that tearing down others can inflate ourselves. Yet the underlying message is something like, *I wouldn't think of doing such a thing,* or *I could never do that* or *I am shocked and aghast at such behavior.* We are usually noting how utterly different we are from these people or how we would simply never sink to their level. Criticizing others is not just an offensive move against them; it is also a defensive move to protect our own "purity."

When we are judgmental, therefore, we *need* other people's faults in order to dodge our own. Stated simply, judgmental thinking is addicted to other people's faults or destructive behavior. Judgmentalism finds its identity in what it *is not.* It defines itself by what it is reacting against. If there were no one around to condemn, judgmentalism wouldn't know what to do with itself.

The judgments we hold about specific issues need to come from a larger context of care and love. While we cannot possibly *feel* the same toward all people, we are asked to *act* lovingly regardless of the level of affection we may or may not have toward them. Acting with love and being judgmental are mutually opposed to each other. Seeing the dignity beneath obnoxious behavior, recognizing the irreducible value of all people and caring for the person beneath the unfair ideas is an enormous challenge. Our only hope, in my estimation, is to regularly remind ourselves of the grace that has been given to us and to allow that grace to extend outward. Roberta Bondi sums this up very well:

> Loving can be difficult business. It is impossible to grit the teeth and love, no matter how much we may want to. That is because human effort is only one of the two basic elements necessary for the fulfillment of all Christian goals and desires, but particularly for love. The other is God's grace. Without grace, nothing is possible.[2]

2

MAKING JUDGMENTS WITHOUT BEING JUDGMENTAL

I remember overhearing a conversation at a party that called my attention to the difference between "making judgments" and "being judgmental." Two people were talking: Bill mentioned to Brad that a young girl he knew had been sexually abused. Bill was ethically outraged and stunned that this event had happened. "Can you believe this?" he said. "I know that little girl!" Bill went on to declare, "I really hope they catch the pervert!"

Brad then said, "You don't really know what may have been going on with the perpetrator. Perhaps he was sexually abused also. Perhaps he couldn't help what he did. You really shouldn't be judgmental about what he did."

"Not be judgmental!" yelled Bill. "How can I possibly be nonjudgmental, Brad? Are you saying that what he did was okay?"

"That's not for me to say," responded Brad. "Things just happen. Who are we to judge them? I'm part of a spiritual discussion group that believes we should judge nothing. Surely none of us is in a position to judge."

This conversation revealed a profound confusion about the differences between making judgments and being judgmental. Brad confused the notion of judgmentalism with making ethical judgments about hurtful, life-damaging behavior. The *behavior* of the perpetrator indeed needs to be judged. Who *really* believes we should be "neutral" or "open-minded" about sexual abuse? No one, I hope. It's wrong. It's a terrible violation of another person, a young vulnerable person. By refusing to judge this act, Brad was essentially ignoring its ethical consequences. The perpetrator is surely a complicated human being, and the perpetrator's entire being and existence should not be leveled because of this act. Yet whatever the context, this act was *wrong and needed to be judged.*

Many of us confuse the difference between making judgments and being judgmental. Yet the two mental processes are not at all the same. Again, it is perfectly appropriate to negatively evaluate actions and behavior that bring hurt, damage or pain to another person. In fact, to *not* react to such a behavior is to have a numbed sense of conscience. A world without judgments would be a world without conviction, principles and ethical concerns. Regardless of how flexible and open-minded we may want to be, we cannot have a concept of "the good life" without a picture of what is detrimental and destructive to that good life.

Therefore, in retaliation against judgmentalism some individuals have insisted on judging nothing. All things, they say, are acceptable or somehow a part of the scheme of things. All of us have our private opinions, but someone else's behavior is none of our business. The worst thing imaginable is intolerance. In fact, intolerance is seen as the only taboo in a very diverse world. Hence, we don't want to be seen as someone who makes "judgments." However, regardless of what we may *claim* in a group discussion, we cannot live our lives completely value-neutral. Our values reside beneath every decision we make. We may not be aware of it at the time, but our values are constantly guiding our behavior.

If we do embrace a judge-nothing philosophy, however, the end result is ethical neutrality and moral indifference. A desire to not come down on anything places us in a world without convictions, a place where all standards are completely private, and in a situation in which society is nearly impossible. One morality is just as good as the next. The confusion here results from not separating the judgment of behaviors from the judgment of entire people. And this separation is notoriously hard to do. Again, some behaviors need very much to be judged. They are damaging to people and harmful to life. They deteriorate the well-being of this world. They are destructive and in some cases evil. Yet this focus on behaviors must be kept separate from a denouncement of entire people. Let's look, more specifically, at the differences between making judgments and being judgmental.

HEALTHY JUDGMENT VS. JUDGMENTALISM

I want to suggest seven very important distinctions between the necessary process of making judgments and the unnecessary process of being judgmental. Let's examine each of them in table 2.1 and the sections below.

Concern. Whereas healthy judgment involves concern for others, judgmentalism often has no concern whatsoever for the people it is condemning. Judgmentalism does not care if it hurts another's feelings; it is far more interested in winning the argument than in helping another human being. The irony for judgmentalism is that people will not listen, no matter how convincing the argument, if they do not feel cared for.

These, then, are some of the principal contrasts between healthy judgment and judgmentalism. Healthy judgment evaluates evidence carefully; is unafraid to decide; recognizes its own limitations; is willing to change its mind; refuses to distrust another's motives unless

Table 2.1. Seven Distinctions Between Healthy Judgment and Judgmentalism

Healthy Judgment	Judgmentalism
Healthy judgment involves concern for others. (Concern)	Judgmentalism is not concerned for others.
Healthy judgment refuses to distrust another's motives unless it has solid evidence for doing so. (Trust)	Judgmentalism presumes to know other people's motives without reasonable evidence.
Healthy judgment involves holding to moral and religious concepts with charity and tolerance toward those who differ. (Tolerant)	Judgmentalism clings tenaciously to moral and religious concepts with disrespect and intolerance toward those who differ.
Healthy judgment entails a denunciation of hurtful *behavior* or erroneous *ideas*. (Behavior vs. People)	Judgmentalism denounces the *person* who adheres to erroneous ideas or destructive behavior.
Healthy judgment recognizes the unresolved problems with its own viewpoints. It has learned that it can have conviction without having certainty, thus being open to other perspectives. (Open)	Judgmentalism refuses to recognize problems or limitations with its own viewpoint. It insists on absolute certainty.
Healthy judgment is the rational process of evaluating evidence and coming to well-thought-out decisions. (Time)	Judgmentalism is emotional reasoning, which makes snap decisions based on superficial evidence.
Healthy judgment is the necessary outcome of reflective, careful thinking and the mark of a mind unafraid to decide. (Unafraid)	Judgmentalism is the outcome of unreflective, careless thinking and is the mark of a mind afraid to think analytically.

there is clear evidence for this suspicion; holds its convictions with charity and tolerance for others; separates behavior and ideas from the people who hold them; and involves a concern for others. These features are typically lacking in judgmentalism.

Trust. Another characteristic of healthy judgment is that it refuses to distrust another's motives unless we have solid evidence for doing so. Judgmentalism, on the other hand, claims to be able to read people's minds. Judgmentalism *knows* what everyone's motive is, even when there is no reasonable evidence. It has secret information, which it uses to clobber another. Judgmentalism, therefore, is highly suspicious, if not paranoid, of others. It doesn't give anybody the benefit of the doubt. For instance, when someone does something nice for us, he or she must be after something. When a man and woman talk, they must be planning an affair. Notice the arrogance involved in the claim to know all these things about people.

Much of this mentality emerges, I believe, from a fearful preoccupation that others are trying to take advantage of us. Instead of admitting our fears, we project them onto others whose motives we then demonize. Because of our own anxiety, we claim to know intuitively what others are secretly thinking, planning or plotting. This is our way of feeling safe. The sad reality is that we are trying to feel safe by prematurely identifying enemies when they may be potential friends.

Tolerant. Another characteristic of judgmentalism is that it often clings so tenaciously to religious and moral concepts that it ends up disrespecting anyone who is different. Healthy judgment may indeed think that the ideas of someone are off-base, limited or even dangerous. However, it extends tolerance to the *person* beneath the *ideas.* It knows that giving an opposing viewpoint air time does not mean that it endorses it. Judgmentalism, on the other hand, is afraid to even hear another perspective. It cannot distinguish between respectfully listening to people and agreeing with them. When we are judgmental, we often become paranoid about ideas different from our own. Superstitiously, we assume that merely hearing these ideas will somehow cause us to be taken over by them. Out of fear, we disregard common courtesy. While healthy judgment is not afraid to condemn racism, sexism, dehumanizing attitudes, the exploitation of people and other destructive practices, judgmentalism refuses to separate the person from their ideas and conduct.

Behavior vs. people. A woman once told me that she had decided to see her minister to talk about the possibility of leaving her husband. Her husband, she said, was regularly abusing her physically, verbally and emotionally. She tended to be passive, easygoing and "too" forgiving. Finally gathering the inner strength to admit that she wanted more out of life than this abuse, she made an appointment with her pastor. As she began to explain the history and complexity of her relationship—especially talking about how her own family-of-origin experiences may have led her toward an abusive relationship—she noticed that the minister seemed rather uninterested. Observing this, she asked the pastor, "Am I being clear?"

"Yes," said the pastor, "but I have only one question."

"Okay," she said, "please ask me."

"Has your husband been unfaithful? Has he had an affair?"

"No," she said, "not that I'm aware of."

"Then you have no grounds for a divorce," pronounced the minister. "You need to stay with this man and work it out. In fact, you must not have a very strong sense of commitment! If there's been no infidelity, then you need to pray and work harder in the relationship."

When I first heard about this story, this was the immediate, judgmental monologue inside my own head: *This story is offensive on so many fronts! Here's a pastoral "counselor" who sizes up this woman's entire marriage in ten minutes. He reduces every complexity in her life and demands that it fit his marital categories. He refuses to struggle with her, to understand her, to explore the unknown with her. In short, he refuses to be bothered by her! This is one of the ugliest psychological sins one human being can do to another—reducing her entire, complex world into something quite manageable for him. He is not very pastoral, and he is certainly not a counselor. His fundamentalist, black-and-white standards are willing to send this woman back into a highly abusive marriage. Maybe he has a lousy marriage and wants everyone else to be unhappy, also. He's just another rigid and uptight fanatic who can't deal with life.*

I don't know who was more judgmental—me or the minister. Yes, he was certainly not hearing the complexities of her life and seemed more preoccupied with his "answer" than with genuinely hearing her struggles. He seemed to approach this problem with a rather black-and-white framework, which did not do justice to the woman's life experience. Yes, he was more interested in sizing up the situation from an outsider's view than with empathizing with her dilemma and pain. Yet what was I doing? The same thing! She told me about this guy, and I had him placed within a belligerent fanatic category without even meeting him. He was nothing but a fundamentalist to me. From there, I made all sorts of caricatures about his personality and stereotyped him with an authoritarian, rigid, dogmatic label. I didn't simply think he mishandled her feelings, I thought he was a lousy minister and human being. How proud I was to point out *his* self-righteousness.

While I do not think that this pastor's approach on *that* particular day with *that* particular person was very effective or caring, I had no business jumping to the conclusion that there was not a caring bone in the man's body. Further, while I don't think his premature advice was beneficial to her, this hardly means that he was operating with a sinister motive to heighten her misery. Yes, I think the man was wrong, but I should not judge his entire ministry or personhood based on one situation. I was accusing him of evaluating this woman's life without any sense of empathy, yet where was *my* empathy when I attacked his entire life? Again, this is the insidiousness of judgmentalism: We can often become very judgmental in our fight against judgmentalism.

Open. Healthy judgment also recognizes the unresolved problems with our own viewpoints. We realize that we'll never have everything figured out *perfectly*, but in the meantime, we can live full lives. Healthy judgment recognizes its limits without shame or self-ridicule. It does not parade its view as if that view had no problems. It admits having blinders or areas in which it does not see the whole picture. It has learned that it can have conviction without having certainty.

Nonjudgmentalism is willing to risk the journey into another person's world, which always means the possibility that we may be changed too. Henri Nouwen, in his typical eloquence, states this beautifully:

> No one can help anyone without becoming involved, without entering with his whole person into the painful situation, without taking the risk of becoming hurt, wounded or even destroyed in the process. . . . Who can save a child from a burning house without the risk of being hurt by the flames? Who can listen to a story of loneliness and despair without taking the risk of experiencing similar pains in his own heart and even losing his precious peace of mind? In short: "Who can take away suffering without entering it?"[1]

By contrast, judgmentalism refuses to recognize any problems or limitations with its own viewpoint. With intellectual arrogance, it insists on absolute certainty. If it is challenged, it frequently reacts with hostility toward the questioner. It is proud of its conviction and expects immediate agreement from others.

Healthy judgment also involves a willingness to change one's mind. This means that right in the middle of an argument, we may turn about face and say, "I believe you're right." While we may not see this happen very often, it *is* a possibility when we form healthy judgments. We simply see that another viewpoint explains more or makes more sense than ours, perhaps because we have taken the time to enter into another person's world. Because we are not arrogantly attached to "owning" the truth, we are then free to change our thinking as new evidence comes in. This does *not* mean that we lack convictions, nor does it mean that we have previously been an idiot. It simply means that we have new information, a new perspective, a better way of looking at something than before. In short, this kind of change is quite possible if we can keep our swollen and bruised egos out of the picture.

Consider the following example. Henry frequently drank coffee at a local café with several other retired men who enjoyed gathering together every morning. While the conversation touched on many topics, it often came back around to politics. Some of the men enjoyed hearing each other's opinions, and while they sometimes disagreed, it was usually an invigorating discussion. Henry, however, was another matter! The group was often sabotaged from interesting conversation because Henry could not stand anyone who disagreed with him. Even if another person had a more sensible argument, more evidence and differed with Henry in a friendly manner, Henry would dig in and want to argue the rest of the day. Henry always had more opinions than facts, stronger emotions than reasons. Many of these gatherings were forfeited by Henry's fierce need to argue. He was like a dog with a bone, unable to let anything go. If the group tried to change topics, Henry would bring it back to his argument. He would get so red-faced that some members of the group feared that he was going to have a heart attack right in the café. Henry was a conversation stopper. When the rest of the group saw him come in, they knew that this was the end of a good conversation. He came each morning not to hear, share or understand better; instead, he came to push his opinions on everyone else and get some sort of hostile delight out of arguing with people. Henry wasn't going to change his mind about anything! Eventually, the group started meeting at another place in hopes that Henry would not discover where they were.

Most of us have met a "Henry" before. A stubborn refusal to change one's mind often promotes a relentless argumentativeness that is difficult for others to endure. The challenge is to stand for our convictions while not resorting to argumentative reactivity, which will alienate us from people. We may ask ourselves, "Why do I take the bait?" But the answer is that it is extremely difficult not to take it.

Time. While being open to new information and other perspectives, making a healthy judgment involves a calm, sober insistence on looking at all the evidence before reaching a conclusion. Healthy judgments normally take *time*. They are weighed out, evaluated and thought about carefully. Healthy judgments attempt to nondiscriminately examine as many factors as possible. They refuse to make mental jumps or careless castigations.

Stated simply, careful judgments are the opposite of snap decisions. Snap decisions are usually promoted by a sudden burst of reactionary emotion. We quickly shuffle someone into a stereotype, or we rapidly place a concept in with "all those other weird ideas" we've heard before. When we meet someone new, we are immediately ready to categorize: redneck, egghead, highbrow, lowbrow, radical feminist, chauvinist, religious nut, heathen and so on.

If a problem or issue does not trigger a great deal of emotion, most of us are capable of making healthy judgments. A decision as to which school to attend, which house to buy or which insurance policy is best are all familiar examples. We *want* to be cautious and conscientious.

Judgmentalism as a mentality, however, is based on reactionary protest to something. It is emotional reasoning, which allows clear thinking no room to navigate amidst our colliding feelings. It does not seem to care that it lacks solid evidence. It is a knee-jerk opinion. Much of the time, this emotional reasoning is based on some sort of unfairness or hurt we have experienced in the past. Someone then says or does something that triggers this unpleasant memory, and we automatically strike out or want to write them off. This is often done instantly and unconsciously. Our ability to listen to people and evaluate their perspectives is hijacked by our emotional reaction. All of a sudden we are fighting old battles that sometimes have little to do with the present issue. We are recycling unhealed resentments and injuries from our personal past.

An example of this can be taken from my psychology classes. When Sigmund Freud is introduced, some students almost immediately recoil. Freud, for them, is both a chauvinist and a man utterly preoccupied with sex. Because of his evaluation of women, the man has no truth to speak whatsoever! Even his name conjures up emotional reactions. The conclusion is drawn that because he had *some* sexist attitudes, *all* of his theories are invalid and not worth investigating. Freud is dismissed even before his ideas are understood.

This also happens frequently when we get into a new romantic relationship, particularly if we have not had adequate time to grieve and let go of a previous relationship. Jenny decided that she could not deal with Alan's perpetually irresponsible lifestyle any longer. He was quite undependable and she wanted a partner she could count on. Her friends encouraged her to eventually go out with Brent, whom they said she would really like. Brent arranged a blind date. Because of unexpected traffic problems, Brent was eight minutes late picking Jenny up. She got in the car and immediately told him that she didn't appreciate his lack of consideration and his insensitivity. "I'm only interested," she said, "in people I can count on." This date did not go well. Brent received a lot of heat that belonged to a previous relationship. With unresolved previous hurts, Jenny was poised and ready to place Brent in the "undependable" category. She sized him up within the first five minutes of the date (or I should say in the eight minutes she waited for him). Jenny was not free to evaluate the relationship for its potential and promise. Instead, a snap judgment based on yesterday's experience pushed Brent away.

Unafraid. And finally, another characteristic of healthy judgments is that they are not driven by fear. Instead, they are a careful expression of a mind that, while open to other information, is unafraid to decide based on the information it has. It does not remain forever suspended because it is willing to admit that choosing one thing means denying another. Going to San Francisco on vacation means not going to Florida. Going to a movie means not going to the ballgame. Decision means letting go of some possibilities while affirming others. Healthy judgment is aware that we can't have it all.

Judgmentalism, on the other hand, is driven by fear of carefully examining evidence and thinking analytically. Judgmentalism is too impulsive to carefully look at all the choices. It tends to be unreflective and careless. Again, it does not have time to withhold its opinion; that's too much work and requires too much energy. Instead, it seeks quick black-or-white extremes. Every situation must involve a *right* decision and a *wrong* one. There is no room for ambivalence. It cannot possibly be that there may be three right decisions or *no* right decision. A judgmental mentality expects that life present itself in all-or-nothing categories. It's much too frightening to admit that there may be several angles on a decision. There must be only one!

If we are struggling with a difficult decision, a decision that is complex, murky and requires a great deal of consideration, we will find little help from judgmental people. They can't seem to hold their stallions of judgment back long enough to hear a problem laid out. Before we have even attempted to describe a problem, they have cut us off and given us only two options. These people, however well-intended they may be, make terrible counselors. They simply don't have tolerance for confusion. It's tunnel vision with no capacity to hear ambiguities.

This is why many people seek out professional counselors; they don't go to the counselor to get more advice—they already have plenty of that!—they need help sorting through complex problems. They need someone with the mental space in their head to hear them out, to let them struggle, to look at all angles. They need to have their complexity respected. They do *not* need to have a complicated world painted in black and white.

CRITICAL THINKING VS. THINKING CRITICALLY

Another way of understanding the differences between making judgments and being judgmental is to highlight the differences between critical thinking and thinking critically. Critical thinking is an important skill for the purposes of making judgments. Most colleges have courses that help students develop these critical thinking skills. But by *critical* thinking, I mean *careful* thinking, rather than *negative* thinking. Thinking critically, on the other hand, invokes the mentality of judgmentalism. It is cynical, nonaffirming, and preoccupied with the errors in what another says rather than in the truth in what they are saying. It is not simply careful; instead, it is highly suspicious and even paranoid. Its major concern is faultfinding. To better understand judgmental vs. nonjudgmental thinking, in table 2.2 are some key differences between critical thinking and thinking critically.

Table 2.2. Ten Features of Critical Thinking vs. Thinking Critically

Critical Thinking	Thinking Critically
Critical thinking is a rational process of dispassionate evaluation.	Thinking critically is an emotional process of hostile judgmentalism.
Critical thinking praises and affirms as well as corrects and critiques.	Thinking critically looks for things to condemn and dismiss.
Critical thinking is coolheaded and patient, having no need to rush to judgment.	Thinking critically is hotheaded and impulsive, speedily rushing to judgment.
Critical thinking is able to separate ideas from personalities in order to assess ideas for their own merit.	Thinking critically lumps ideas and personalities together in condemning characterization.
Critical thinking attempts scrupulously to be fair in its representation of ideas with which one disagrees.	Thinking critically creates caricatures, sweeping generalizations and straw men.
Critical thinking is the ability to resist emotional reasoning.	Thinking critically is emotional reactivity masquerading as rationality.
Critical thinking distinguishes between the critical and the hypercritical.	Thinking critically believes that caustic and pedantic faultfinding equals critical thinking.
Critical thinking knows when to cease thinking critically.	Thinking critically is restless until it demolishes.
Critical thinking accepts realities not accessible to or processed by reason.	Thinking critically forces rationalism upon the non-rational until it denies the emotional, intuitive, aesthetic and spiritual.
Critical thinking is able to critique itself.	Thinking critically assumes the product of critical thought is above criticism.

These differences point toward two mentalities. While most of us fluctuate back and forth between the two, it is important to identify times when we are thinking critically rather than looking at something with clear-minded, careful attention. Thinking critically is usually generated not by caution, but instead by sarcasm, cynicism and, ultimately, nihilism. It assumes that affirming anything only indicates how naïve we are. Yet what is interesting is that many people who engage in thinking critically never put their own negativity on trial. Perhaps they feel safer when they believe in nothing.

Yet the belief in nothing is a very important belief and one they should also critically examine. Thinking critically *needs* to be critically examined.

REFLECTIVE AND OPEN-MINDED VS. SOUND BITES AND CLICHÉS

Quite frankly, it is much easier to be down on everything than to affirm something. It requires far less mental and emotional energy. Again, judgmentalism is *easy*, while nonjudgmentalism is difficult and requires a lot of effort. While I wish to strongly encourage open-mindedness throughout this book, I must honestly say that closed-mindedness is far simpler. It may be less fulfilling, but it is more convenient. While clear-minded people may have an understanding of several viewpoints, this awareness of multiple views may make them hesitant, careful and at times even timid. We are, after all, normally less prone toward zealous claims when we notice that there are a lot of perspectives available. In other words, the more we fairly examine alternative positions, the more inclined we may be to doubt ourselves. Author Daniel Taylor is quite frank about the pros and cons of being a reflective, open-minded thinker:

> The life of a reflective person is more likely to be interesting, less likely to be serene; more likely to be contemplative, less likely to be active; more likely to be marked by the pursuit of answers, less by the finding of them. The result is a high potential for creativity, curiosity and discovery, but also for paralyzing

ambivalence, alienation and melancholy.[2]

The point seems to be that we pay a price for greater understanding. Another disadvantage of open-minded thinking is the loss of colorful expletives and inflammatory language. Judgmental language is powerful language. It makes us feel strong when we use it. It is, after all, the vehicle of shame. It is also deceptive in that it makes us believe we are as certain as we sound.

Fair, nonjudgmental language, on the other hand, is less interesting. It tends to be calm, sober and careful about the words it chooses. It forces us to use our minds and not simply rely on strong emotion. It doesn't pulverize anyone. It does not draw a lot of oohs and ahs from an audience. Nonjudgmental language will not rely on inflammatory sound bites, regardless of how much attention that might attract. In short, it refuses to go for the jugular.

It is a sad fact that our public discourse so often revolves around irrational exaggeration and hype. In order to make a point, we often must grossly overstate the point. Especially in any campaign year, just listen to the bombastic words and grandiose zeal of many politicians. The careful, respecting attitude that sees some legitimacy in another's opposing view is completely lost. It's a rigid, mud-slinging world of easy right-and-wrong answers. Being accurate is far less important than being colorful.

"Sound bites," those quick, fiery expressions that squeeze complex issues into trite clichés, are unfortunately appealing to many. This is the world of easy pronouncements and generalizations. These bumper-sticker phrases help many come across very well on televised talk shows and media events. A person who makes a sincere attempt to address all sides of the issue is either cut off or brushed aside as wishy-washy and lacking in convictions. We don't have time to hear that person out.

Often, in the public's view, a person who can memorize a series of provocative words and images, who can aggressively push the discussion back to his or her own limited view, "wins" many debates. Comprehension and depth of understanding get in the way! That's not exciting enough. Instead, we want 100 percent conviction about complicated issues.

But to be loud doesn't mean that someone is profound. To be colorful doesn't mean that someone has understanding. To "call it like it is" may mean that someone has a very narrow view of the world. To be boisterous, overconfident and dogmatic doesn't mean that someone has the truth.

There is a close proximity between judgmentalism and arrogance. In order to better understand judgmentalism and to begin to move away from it in our own thinking, it is important to understand this connection between judmentalism and mental grandiosity. It is to this issue that we now turn.

3

INSECURE ARROGANCE VS. CONFIDENT HUMILITY

Insecure arrogance? Confident humility? Aren't those word combinations completely incompatible? Not according to a friend of mine who is fond of saying, "I'm an egomaniac with an inferiority complex." Actually, I'd like to suggest that there may be far more truth in this statement than we might assume. In this chapter, I will explore the relationship between insecurity, arrogance and judgmentalism. Conversely, I will examine the relationship between humility and confidence, arguing that these terms are quite compatible.

Judgmentalism often comes across as cocksure of itself. When I become judgmental, grandiosity takes over my thinking and I forget Henri Nouwen's words: "The mystery of one man is too immense and too profound to be explained by another man."[1] I somehow claim a complete vision that allows me a total assessment of another person. This mentality is profoundly arrogant and full of itself. Who am I to think that I have the mental equipment to completely evaluate another human being? How did I manage to step outside of my own mental filters and life experience to find a place of Godlike objectivity from which to size up an entire person?

One of the problems with arrogant thinking is that it no longer sees any need for empathy. It already knows the whole truth, so why bother with deeply hearing another perspective? Perhaps one of the central features of judgmental thinking is that it always lacks empathy. Empathy, as psychologist Carl Rogers points out so well, is that capacity to enter another's viewpoint and understand life from that angle.[2] It is primarily a cognitive exercise. While it involves understanding someone's feelings, it is essentially a mental process of deep, nonjudgmental listening in which we risk taking on another person's perspective.

Empathy does *not* mean approving of all aspects of another's beliefs or behavior. It does, however, necessitate giving the perspective air time and listening with new ears and fewer preconceived ideas. But there are profound risks in developing a lifestyle of empathic listening. We may be significantly moved by another person's perspective. We may walk away from the conversation with far less certainty than we had before. Whatever the results, however, we will feel the fulfillment of having respected the person in spite of his or her destructive behavior.

Another arrogant aspect of judgmentalism is that it understands only its own viewpoint. In a sense, judgmental thinking is intoxicated with its own perspective. When I am the most judgmental, I am not really able to think freely. It is not so much that I have rigid thoughts; instead, rigid thoughts seem to *have me!* I become a prisoner of my own thinking, unable to get outside, underneath or beyond it enough to see with comprehension. I am unreachable, drunk on the wine of my own certainty.

This inability to take on other perspectives creates enormous limits in our relationships with others. Most of us have had the experience of trying to talk with a person who will not even attempt to see our angle on things. This, of course, can be enormously frustrating.

The annoyance is not so much that another person disagrees with us, but rather, that they won't even hear us in the first place. Our outlook is simply not given a chance. They believe that recognizing any legitimacy to our viewpoint automatically means giving up their own. Consequently, no value is seen in anything we are trying to say.

Perspective-taking may well be one of the most important relationship skills we can ever develop. When we are completely absorbed by our own vision of things, we obviously cannot benefit from anybody else's angle. Perspective-taking moves us away from the arrogance of thinking we have a monopoly on reality.

But it is now time to ask a central question concerning the relationship between arrogance and judgmentalism: Does arrogance represent a *primary* problem? Are self-exaltation and conceit the most basic underlying factors contributing to judgmentalism? It certainly appears that way at times, but is there something deeper going on? More specifically, what is the relationship between arrogance and insecurity?

THE CONTROVERSIAL ISSUE OF SELF-ESTEEM

In a previous book, *Sin, Pride & Self-Acceptance,* I examined two opposing perspectives concerning the issue of self-esteem.[3] One perspective, rooted in Augustine's conviction that pride is the root problem of the human condition, argues that human beings have an inclination to *overvalue,* rather than *undervalue,* themselves. In other words, we tend to inflate ourselves. We often believe that we are better than we are. In fact, many social psychologists such as David Myers describe this tendency as a *self-serving bias.*[4] In fact, there is a very impressive body of research that suggests that human beings credit themselves when they do well and blame others when they fail. Self-evaluations are highly skewed in a favorable light. Students believe that if they get As in a class, they have earned them, but if their grades are poor, either the test or the professor was not fair. In turn, professors tend to overrate their own performances, with large percentages believing that they are among the best academics on campus. In one study, 94 percent of college faculty saw themselves as better than the average colleague.[5] Myers believes that these studies in social psychology reaffirm the old Augustinian position that we think too much, rather than too little, of ourselves. A self-serving, self-justifying tendency clouds our reason. As Myers puts it, "Although it is popularly believed that most people suffer from the 'I'm not OK-You're OK' syndrome, research indicates that William Saroyan was much closer to the truth: 'Every man is a good man in a bad world—as he himself knows.'"[6] For Myers, a more accurate diagnosis of the human condition is that we suffer from a *superiority* complex rather than an *inferiority* one:

> Note how radically at odd this conclusion is with the popular wisdom that most of us suffer from low self-esteem and high self-disparagement. We are, to be sure, strongly motivated to maintain and enhance our self-esteem and we will welcome the message which helps us do that. But most of us are not groveling about with feelings that everyone else is better than we are. Preachers who deliver ego-boosting pep talks to audiences who are supposedly plagued with miserable self-images are preaching to a problem that seldom exists.[7]

Myers *does* believe that some people suffer from low self-esteem. These are the ones prone to show up at a therapist's office. But therapists then frequently overgeneralize this problem and believe it is descriptive of most people. In fact, these therapists have led a pop-psychology movement, which has suggested that low self-esteem is the *primary problem* of the human condition. For Myers, this is both bad science and a highly unfortunate message, which leads our culture to think that we undervalue, rather than overvalue, ourselves. This highly limited number of patients with low self-esteem hardly describes the general population.

So Myers wants to utilize this social psychology research to confirm the older Augustinian premise that pride is the primary sin. Our natural inclination is to be too favorable in our self-estimation, to think that we are better than we are. If this is the bottom line, then we should take at face value the arrogance involved in judgmental thinking. People *really do* see themselves in this exalted way.

But the question is whether the research of social psychologists tells the whole story about self-esteem. Many clinical psychologists, psychotherapists and psychoanalysts believe that it does *not*. The problem, they argue, is with the nature of the social psychology research. These findings come largely from questionnaires and interviews that only deal with the surface of what people think about themselves. For many therapists, these surface self-affirmations do not reveal what may be occurring beneath this flattering self-report. In other words, saying positive things about oneself to an interviewer and having a deeply rooted high self-regard may be two different things. Often people tell us what they think they *should* say or how they'd *like* to feel about themselves. But all of this, according to many clinical psychologists, can be a compensation for underlying feelings that are not flattering at all. And why do these clinicians frequently say this? Because in working with people in psychotherapy, they frequently have the opportunity to get behind these defenses and see that arrogance is often a cover for deep insecurity. Beneath the exalted self is a highly vulnerable, shaky and insecure self. So while social psychologists are doing surface research with many, psychotherapists are doing much deeper research with a few. So they trust their own findings and not the results of questionnaires.

The key issue here is the significance of the unconscious. For many psychotherapists and all psychoanalysts, the unconscious realm is always working behind the scenes. There is probably a history of narcissistic injury and woundedness beneath what appears to be conceit. Under most bragging is unconscious self-doubt, and under most displays of superiority is a nagging sense of inadequacy. A psychoanalyst would say to a social psychologist, "Of course, out of their defensiveness and compensatory behavior, research subjects are going to *tell* you that they like themselves. But this does not mean they really do."

This controversy has to do with different research methods and fundamentally different views of the psyche. If the "pride is primary" group claims Augustinian theological roots, perhaps the "low self-esteem" group could claim theological roots in Irenaeus, who saw the human dilemma more in terms of insecurity and immaturity than arrogance and pride. Evangelicals, as general rule, have been much more influenced by the Augustinian argument. Further, at least in my mind, evangelicals have produced better academic and research psychologists than they have psychotherapists. Put another way, they haven't paid a lot of attention to the unconscious. In fact, many evangelical therapy styles have focused on conscious reason as the backbone of mental health. Cognitive therapy is popular. Many mainline denominations, on the other hand, have been much more influenced by depth psychology. Historically, the American Association of Pastoral Counselors, a dominantly mainline group, has had a long courtship with psychoanalysis. Unfortunately, there has not been much ecumenical dialogue between mainliners and evangelicals. Evangelicals have produced some excellent scholars, particularly in the psychology and theology dialogue, as well as in the dialogue between philosophy of science and psychology. Some mainliners have also offered interesting theological evaluations of various forms of psychotherapy. Roman Catholics have a rich tradition of connecting spiritual development to the process of psychotherapy. It is past time for these three groups to listen more attentively to each other.

But in the meantime, what are we to make of this pride versus low self-esteem debate and its relevance for our topic of judgmentalism? I believe that we can be enormously helped with this issue when we look at the thought of Karen Horney, who consistently argued that pride and self-contempt are actually two sides of the same coin.[8] While interested readers may want to check my development of this theme in *Sin, Pride & Self-Acceptance*, I will not repeat the argument here. However, I do wish to mention some of Horney's main points.

Horney readily accepts the psychoanalytic point that a great deal of insecurity and even self-contempt often underlie our grandiose exhibitionism. In fact, she often points out that the word "arrogance" comes from the word *arrogate*, which has to do with attributing something to ourselves that we really do not possess. Thus, she rather brilliantly develops the notion that healthy self-esteem and neurotic pride (arrogance) are *very* different. Beneath arrogance is a fragile self, a shaky self, which covers its fragility with grandiose claims and neurotic pride. Yet Horney offers an additional insight. Just as insecurity lies behind self-inflation, so self-inflation lies behind what appears to be low self-esteem.

In other words, we are often extremely down on ourselves because an unconscious pride system tells us that we ought to match our idealized self. If I am perpetually self-berating, I may need to look at the implicit (and arrogant!) assumptions with which I operate. Perhaps I expect to be above the traffic of ordinary human problems, immune

Table 3.1. Confident Humility vs. Insecure Arrogance

Confident Humility	Insecure Arrogance
Confident humility is based on a realistic assessment of itself.	Insecure arrogance is based on imaginary qualities it claims to have.
Confident humility pursues goals in harmony with its true being and actual potential.	Insecure arrogance creates a false self that relentlessly searches for praise.
Confident humility is based on qualities of character.	Insecure arrogance wants to parade accomplishments, attainments or relationships for their prestige value.
Confident humility needs connection more than worshipers and accepts faults and limitations as part of being human.	Insecure arrogance claims inflated virtues but needs a constant audience and feels outraged at inattention.
Confident humility identifies with the common human condition.	Insecure arrogance demands special favor and privilege.
Confident humility accepts moral responsibility and the need for forgiveness.	Insecure arrogance minimizes and justifies its moral flaws.
Confident humility is able to acknowledge and appreciate the accomplishments of others.	Insecure arrogance feels enormous envy and disdain toward others who accomplish things.
Confident humility is not afraid to look at its dark side.	Insecure arrogance denies its own problems and projects them off onto someone else.
Confident humility is not afraid to embrace reality.	Insecure arrogance is far more concerned with image than reality.
Confident humility accepts vulnerability as part of the human package.	Insecure arrogance hates vulnerability and tries desperately to cover it up.
Confident humility accepts responsibility for its own actions.	Insecure arrogance explains away and blames others for failure.

from the struggles that others experience. While it sounds nearly brutal to say this, people with chronic low self-esteem may be working with an implicit pride system that demands that they be better than everyone else. This is why Horney frequently argues that pride and self-contempt are two sides of the same coin. While we are quick to notice the insecurity beneath neurotic pride, we are not so quick to notice the neurotic pride beneath self-contempt. But for Horney, both are present.

Because the connection between arrogance and judgmentalism is so crucial, I list some of the key differences between false pride and genuine self-confidence in table 3.1. (Many of these points are derived from Horney's work.)

GRANDIOSITY, SHAME AND NARCISSISM

Over the past several decades, the topic of narcissism has moved from an individual concern to a larger-scale cultural critique of American society. While Christopher Lasch's book *The Culture of Narcissism*[9] probably led the pack in this indictment, other social critics also made important contributions.[10] Narcissism has been understood as a tendency to be self-absorbed, self-inflated and in constant need of adoration and praise. It's built on a framework that says, "It's all about me." It appears self-indulgent, selfish and utterly preoccupied with its own needs. Narcissists are generally incapable of caring about others because all their attention is turned inward. They don't want relationships, they want mirrors; they don't want give-and-take connection, they want an audience. Narcissists feel entitled to special privilege, and they often feel outraged if these narcissistic needs are not met. They appear to have almost no remorse about anything because they are too wonderful to have faults. They also do not have much gratitude, because after all, they are entitled to what they want. Sincere thanks and genuine apologies don't flow from their mouths. Also, narcissists frequently display a vicious envy toward others who accomplish more than they do. In short, narcissism is portrayed as a psychologically ugly condition.

This highly negative view of narcissism has also been part of psychoanalytic history. Freud himself, beginning in 1914, argued that adult narcissists could not be treated with psychoanalysis. Freud believed that each of us is born in a state of "primary narcissism," in which the first object of our libido is ourselves. Babies naturally see themselves as the center of the universe. This egocentricity is perfectly natural. Eventually, however, during the course of healthy development, children turn their attention toward others. For Freud, because we only have a limited amount of libido energy, if we love ourselves, there is normally nothing left for others. If we persist in this self-preoccupation as we grow older, it is called "secondary narcissism." Because psychoanalysis focuses on previous relationships in one's life, and narcissists are only capable of a relationship with themselves, they are not candidates for analysis. They have nothing to "transfer" onto the analyst from previous relationships, so they are not analyzable—and such transference is the means by which analysis is conducted. Thus, even within the early psychoanalytic tradition there has often been a rather condemning attitude of the narcissistic condition.

Again, narcissists appear to have excessive self-regard and to view themselves as perfect specimens. Thus, narcissism and judgmentalism toward others have often been connected. While narcissists need others too much to alienate them completely, they nevertheless often come across in a very self-righteous and condemning manner. It is always someone else's fault. After all, how could it *possibly* be them?

I would like to suggest that the issue of narcissism provides us with an excellent opportunity to see the two-edged sword of judgmentalism. On the one hand, narcissism and arrogant judgmentalism are often teamed up together. Narcissists can be demanding, self-exonerating and highly condemning of other people. Point granted. Yet I would also like to suggest that many of us have become enormously judgmental of narcissists. In other words, we've written them off as hopelessly self-consumed, indulgent, unethical and without redemption. Most descriptions of narcissism end with the sentiment, "yuck!" In other words, narcissists have sometimes become the psychological lepers of our day, the ones for whom we have no compassion. When the word narcissist is used to describe someone, that usually means the person is hopeless, period.

What I'm suggesting is that it is easy for us to moralize about narcissism in such a way that we no longer see the person beneath the condition. Pastoral counselor Donald Capps argues that theologians have, all too easily, jumped on the bandwagon of condemning narcissistic sin without adequately understanding the nature and dynamics of narcissism.[11] Let me state this another way: *As long as we see narcissism as "nothing but arrogance," we will be enormously tempted to treat the narcissist with contempt and misunderstand the deeper reality of his or her condition.* Whether we use religious or psychological labels to condemn someone is not important; *it's still condemnation.* Our condemnation of the narcissist will not address the deeper wounding beneath all the posturing and exhibitionism. Stated another way, what narcissists desperately need is the internalization of grace, a deep sense of acceptance, which can free them from their own painful self-preoccupations.

While there is a strong tendency within Christian thought to understand arrogance as the central and primary sin, there are other resources that can help us see beneath this self-flattery. Kierkegaard, for one, understood that it is impossible to be a human being without feeling a great deal of anxiety. This anxiety concerns our future, the implications of the choices we make, our own limitations and, ultimately, our death. It is impossible to escape this disorienting anxiety. No amount of medication or psychotherapy can eliminate it. While narcissism may *appear* to defy this finitude and live from some exalted plane, the reality is that anxiety, *and therefore insecurity,* persists. The narcissist may be quite good at hiding this underlying insecurity, but this does not mean it has disappeared.

In fact, the narcissist's self-obsession is a clue that something is unsettled within. This anxiety, as Kierkegaard argued so well, is not itself sin, but it is the *precondition* of sin.[12] We can accept our finitude and place our trust in our Creator, or we can frantically try to resolve our insecure plight on the basis of our own devices. Yet like a person in quicksand, the more we try to conquer this basic anxiety, the more we sink into it. By not accepting our anxiety, we place ourselves at the center of our lives and our own ego becomes God: we must master our own fate and control our own destiny. The problem, of course, is that we do not have the ability to wrestle and conquer these ultimate concerns. We may *pretend* that we do (and I would argue that narcissism is always pretentious, not based on solid self-esteem or solid confidence; it is false confidence that has stretched beyond its actual potential), but we actually don't.

This same point can also be seen in the brilliant analysis of the human condition offered by Reinhold Niebuhr. Borrowing heavily from Kierkegaard, Niebuhr also discusses the relationship between anxiety and sin. Niebuhr is known primarily for a rather blistering analysis of the sin of pride and self-exaltation. Niebuhr wrote in a historical period rife with egomaniacal pride and arrogant dictatorship. Yet Niebuhr never lost awareness of the underbelly of this pride. He knew quite well that this pride emerges from an underlying anxiety, ontological insecurity and distrust in God. He hammered away at pride because it was so destructive. Yet Niebuhr's view of pride involved more than a boisterous, loud display of self-mastery. For Niebuhr, pride emerges when people place the solution of their lives in their own hands, rather than trusting in God. At times, this pride may not even *look* like pride. It can take many forms, like the self-castigation because of high personal expectations that I described earlier. While feminist critics of Niebuhr have been right to point out that the sin of excessive self-assertion may be more of a male than a female form of sin, Niebuhr nevertheless understood that pride is closely connected to insecurity and anxiety.

Again, by linking the strange and paradoxical words "insecure arrogance," I am pointing toward not just the obvious arrogance, but to the insecurity that propels that arrogance. To put it another way, I am suggesting that *grandiosity and shame usually travel together.* In other words, the narcissist often moves from feelings of inadequacy, emptiness, incompleteness and even inferiority on the one hand, to compensatory feelings of self-righteousness, pride, contempt for others, vanity and superiority on the other hand. These two poles exist within the narcissist. The point to recognize here is that the grandiose self is also the highly fragile self.

FROM FREUD TO KOHUT

Heinz Kohut, considered by many the most pioneering psychoanalyst since Freud himself, spent most of his adult life exploring narcissism.[13] Unlike Freud, Kohut refused to give up on the narcissist and sought to understand the underlying structure of this self-disorder. While Kohut had a reputation for knowing Freudian theory inside out, at least when it came to narcissism Kohut did not think Freud looked deeply enough.[14]

For Kohut, the classical Freudian approach to narcissism, which sees narcissism as essentially a spoiled condition of entitlement and grandiosity, is ineffective. Kohut believes that the focus on the person's grandiosity is far less significant than a focus on the underlying vulnerability. Kohut does not deny that both are present; he simply believes vulnerability must be addressed first. This grandiosity reveals the presence of earlier narcissistic injury. In other words, the person is somewhat fixated in an earlier developmental period, in which insufficient acknowledgment, affirmation and attention dominated. The narcissistic tendency reveals a craving that has not been met. The narcissist lacks what every child needs: the chance to be exhibitionistic and to have parents mirror back to us who we are. Narcissists' excitements, perceptions and disappointments were not reflected back to them. Consequently, narcissists attempt to get that mirroring from everyone around them.

In fact, the narcissist's experience is often considered unreal unless someone else is watching. In healthy development, children receive this attention, availability and emotional soothing from parents and are therefore later able to soothe themselves. The resources of the parent are digested so that they become the resources of the child. Kohut frequently calls this "transmuting internalizations." In unhealthy development, the grandiose self of childhood never gets to be on stage and perform. And this hunger for mirroring does not go away. It appears in adulthood, often with the expectation that adult relationships are going to meet the needs of a narcissistic child. David Augsburger describes this process very well:

> If the person experiences the subject in the surrounding world as unavailable, nonempathic, and withholding understanding, the hungry self develops voracious narcissistic needs. When the rejection is extreme, the compensation for it by the empty self is also extreme. The unfulfilled needs leave gaps in the formation of the self, missing pieces in the self-structure.[15]

For Kohut, there needs to be a gleam in the sparkling eyes of parents as they empathically respond to the age-appropriate exhibitionism of their children. Put simply, parents need to enjoy watching their children perform and show off. If the self is to grow and develop, this early period of display needs to be mirrored. If this is done, a child will not stay stuck there. Inevitably, parents will fail at empathy, but this gradual empathic failure will not be perceived as catastrophic. Instead, it will provide the optimal frustration by which a child can become more realistic. Children give up the need to be the center of the universe *after* they have had the opportunity to *be* the center of the universe.

Parents also need to be available for children to idealize. When children idealize a parent, they can then feel strong as a result of this identification with that parent. Children need to feel a part of something greater than themselves. By virtue of these connections, children can feel more solid and secure. Kohut believes that it is very important for parents to accept this idealization. Children gain strength from their parents' strength. The idealization will be grandiose at first, but if allowed, it will be later channeled into a more realistic image. Again, part of the strengthening of the self depends on this connection with a larger, stronger self. Put simply, children need to borrow parents' strength on the way to developing their own robust selves. Eventually parents' fallibility will be realized, but for the time, they need to be idealized.

Both the need for mirroring and the need to idealize are part of the child's grandiosity. If development is healthy, this grandiosity is transformed into healthy adult ambitions and motivations. The previously idealized parent becomes an inner resource of guidance and values. Augsburger describes what happens when this does *not* go well:

If these two needs/processes do not go well, the grandiose self, with its exaggerated expectations from the idealized persons, its pretensions to entitlements, its inflated ideas of its own importance, abilities, and power, begins to come apart. When others do not respond with the expected mirroring, approval, and admiration for the "boundless exhibitionism of the grandiose self" then shame results. . . . Narcissism—the self over-concerned with itself—is the self's attempt to substitute self-indulgent self-care for the appropriate care by a significant other which is woefully inadequate. The self-centered behavior of the narcissist arises from too little self-esteem and self-valuation, not from too much. It is the impoverished self that hungrily grasps for attention and affirmation (no matter how smoothly presented or artfully expressed).[16]

Augsburger's comment is loaded with Kohutian insight. The narcissistic self tries in vain to substitute excessive attention and flattery for what was painfully lacking developmentally. But this attempt to make up for the earlier deprivation is doomed to failure. While adult narcissists may occasionally find people who are willing to sacrifice their lives to meet others' narcissistic needs, most adults run out of patience very fast. Narcissists, in their ongoing craving for attention, do not even "see" another person in the room. Others are necessarily devalued as they over-value themselves. Other people are perceived as narcissistic supplies rather than as people in their own right. They are instruments of attention, an audience whose job is to watch them instead of have a life of their own. There is no reciprocity or mutuality in such a relationship.

So to repeat, the parents will gradually and inevitably fail the child's narcissistic needs. This is a part of healthy development. Yet this failure should not be abrupt and disruptive for the child. Kohut often called this gradual withdrawal of narcissistic resources "optimal frustration." This is important because (a) children learn that all of their narcissistic needs cannot be met, and (b) they can learn to be self-soothing without having to always depend on other people to be there. When adults do not have this self-soothing capacity, they express an excessive dependency on others for mirroring and affirmation. This dependency is excessive because they have never developed the resources to take care of themselves. Nothing is real until they "show" someone. This audience-addiction creates enormous pressure for outsiders to be there for the narcissist. The narcissist feels entitled to constant attention, yet this entitlement is fueled by desperation. Without a mirror, they don't have a self. And they don't have the strength to hold up their own mirror.

In working with adult narcissists, Kohut found that empathy, more than confrontational interpretation, is more beneficial. In other words, Kohut allowed the analytic process to replay earlier needs for mirroring and idealization. The focus is on the adult's injurious early psychological environment, rather than on destructive drives that threaten life. This nurturing, mirroring experience addresses the narcissistic injuries that keep patients from moving forward. As Augsburger said, "The goal of empathy is not to remove the other person's problems, but to go beneath them and strengthen the person, to support the growth of a more functional self, to facilitate the movement toward maturation. It is not simply a love cure, but is caring understanding that offers the insight that heals, given in the empathy that cures."[17]

Kohut found that when this empathic immersion is offered, a more robust and realistic sense of self emerges in the narcissist. The analyst, in a sense, does exactly what a healthy parent would have done—namely, provide empathic mirroring and the capacity for idealization. Gradually, the patient realizes that the analyst is not a perfect listener, not omniscient and not always necessary. The patient internalizes some of what the analyst has offered. Initially rebuking patients' grandiosity or challenging their sense of entitlement would have only driven them more deeply into their defenses. It would have in fact promoted narcissistic rage, which is always connected to this deep woundedness.

For Kohut, everyone struggles with narcissism to one degree or another. It is not an us versus them problem. Early narcissistic injuries are primary contributors to most psychological struggles. For instance, Kohut believes that problems with sex and aggression, the two Freudian master motives, are better explained as "disintegrative byproducts."[18] Injuries to the self are deeper than sexual and aggressive conflicts. There is a close connection between the experience of shame and rage. Rather than viewing destructive aggression as part of our biological drives, Kohut sees this aggression as a reaction to narcissistic injury. The same is true of the sex drive. Sexual promiscuity is a *secondary* problem; the deeper issue revolves around a wounded self looking for narcissistic supplies.

It is easy to misunderstand Kohut at this point and think he doesn't offer interpretations to the patient at all. This is not true. But for Kohut, interpretation is an outgrowth of empathy, not a detached, aloof activity made by an emotionally distant analyst. Kohut wants "experience-near" interpretations. In other words, immersing himself in the client's world is a primary method of data collection. In this sense, an empathic approach is a *scientific* approach and not simply a warm and fuzzy way to make the patient feel good. Empathy provides analysts with an understanding that they would normally not have. This vicarious introspection is the appropriate methodology for developing an understanding of the psyche.

Let's expand this point to a general statement: Most of us are not impressed with a confrontation of our behavior by someone who hasn't taken the time to first understand our struggles. Why should we listen to someone who doesn't really know us and has not attempted to grasp our situation? I can point out people's self-centeredness all day long, and it will probably do little good. However, if I listen to them and talk about how their self-preoccupations may be growing out of their own repressed fears and insecurities, they may listen. Even if I am absolutely right about their external self-centered behavior, I have not helped them solve their problem. I need to look deeper. It's easy to moralize from a distance, to preach at rather than speak to someone. Telling people that they are self-centered narcissists will probably only drive them deeper into narcissistic rage.

Again, the more general point is that our prophetic pronouncements need to have been preceded with a caring disposition. I submit that Jesus' challenging critiques of some people would have meant very little if he didn't already have a solid reputation as a caregiver, one capable of showing mercy, kindness and love. If Jesus had simply been a wandering preacher who took every occasion to "tell people the way it is," and to confront their pretentiousness, he would not have inspired his followers to a life of service and care for others. It is easy to tell people off. It makes some feel very righteous, powerful and in control. Yet the intensity of our words, when not matched by the gentleness of our spirit, means almost nothing.

If we are going to act in loving ways toward those who seem quite arrogant and full of themselves, it may be helpful to remember Kohut's description of the injured self beneath all the posturing. If we can listen for the anxious person beneath the conceit, we may be able to respond in more caring ways to such individuals. It certainly won't be easy! Many have developed layers upon layers of defensive pride.

And sometimes, quite frankly, they may need to hear the "law" before grace means much to them. Yet hammering away at the grandiosity, self-elevation and apparent arrogance will probably just drive the person deeper into their denial and false sense of pride. Loving arrogant people is an enormous challenge and one that regularly requires the assistance of God's grace.

HUMBLE SELF-CONFIDENCE

The word *humility* has acquired some unfortunate connotations. As I speak of humility, I am not talking about a self-derogatory attitude, a sense of inferiority or a tendency to be down on oneself. Much of these behaviors, in my opinion, are outward displays to *make people think* that we're humble and have nothing to do with *actually being* humble. Low self-esteem has been confused with humility for far too long.

Humility, instead, comes from a deep recognition of my limitations, faults and internal struggles, but not at the expense of recognizing my gifts, abilities and positive qualities. Humility is a joyful embrace of my humanity—no more, and no less. Humility certainly doesn't mean that I'm the best, but it also takes no glory in the idea that I am the worst. In fact, when I start claiming to be the very worst person, I may very well be experiencing an inverted form of pride. In other words, I may consider myself the champion of the dark side, the person for whom God's love had to work overtime in order to offer me grace. The more I speak openly with other people, however, the more I realize that I have a rather garden-variety dark side. I begin to realize that we are all a mixture of good and bad elements. I am probably no harder or no easier to love than the next guy. I'm on a journey that has been opened up by the grace of God. It is this acceptance, affirmation and love, so often mediated to me by other people, that provides the foundation of my self-confidence. The cultivation of God-given gifts and potentiality sometimes spills over into my own egocentricity. At other times, I may be entirely too down on myself, which itself can be based on a kind of arrogance that I *should* be much better than others and that I am surprised that I struggle as much as others do. When I have humility, I live freely with a deep confidence that I am loved and that all will be okay. When my humility fades, I think it's all about my performance, a performance that will determine my worth and acceptability.

Genuine humility and self-confidence are friends, not enemies. It is actually arrogance that cannot be linked with self-confidence. These two words are inconsistent. Arrogance, as I have explained it, is connected to a false self that makes claims it has no right to make. Self-confidence, on the other hand, emerges from a deep knowledge of our strengths *and* weaknesses. Self-confidence does not waste its energies on fostering an unrealistic self-portrait and the repression of everything that runs counter to that portrait. It is free to invest in life, to develop our potentials and to be grateful to the source of these abilities: God. Self-confidence understands that we are invited into an exciting world of using our potentials to advance human dignity, help each other and promote a more loving world. Humility is in touch with its Source. It doesn't pretend that it has achieved, all on its own, a profound sense of self-acceptance and self-confidence. Instead, humility knows that we are able to accept ourselves because we have been accepted. We need not flex our psychological muscles and brag about how we have completely accepted ourselves; instead, we can smile at a God who alone is able to accept us unconditionally.

A confident humility is also able to acknowledge, appreciate and affirm the gifts and achievements of others. While insecure arrogance is threatened and deeply envious of the abilities of others, humility can enjoy these abilities as the gifts of a fellow traveler. Confident humility does not need to tear apart, criticize or demean the talents of others. Put simply, it is not afraid to compliment others. Insecure arrogance, however, is very stingy with affirmations and only offers them begrudgingly. When I am insecurely arrogant, I see the abilities of others as an attack on my own abilities. In other words, I personalize the achievements of others by saying that their accomplishments are a commentary on my own inadequacy. Rather than focusing on their accomplishments, I'm only reminded of my deficiencies. Because these deficiencies are too painful to face, it is far easier to shoot holes in their accomplishments. By reducing their achievements, I can feel better about myself. Socrates rather famously called envy the daughter of pride, but it is a shallow and shaky pride that feels such intense envy. It is driven by a need to take others down, a rage over not being at center stage, an underlying feeling of inferiority. Envy devalues others in its self-obsessed march to be the best.

Confident humility regularly affirms and values others without a fear that this affirmation will dredge up its own sense of inadequacy. Again, it is sometimes very sad to see how utterly difficult it is for some people to simply compliment another person. I have been astounded by times in which I've seen colleagues provide excellent performances only to receive no positive comments at all from their peers. It is almost as if it is painful for others to affirm them. Confident humility has no problem applauding the abilities of others. It recognizes the uniqueness of everyone and feels no vicious competitive striving. While it does not engage in phony or false affirmation, it regularly lets others know that they are appreciated.

And finally, confident humility is not based on a get-it-quick-and-easy guide to feeling wonderful. I am in complete agreement with

Alan McGinnis when he writes:

> I do not want to give the kind of Pollyanna advice or promote the sort of irresponsible notions one hears from many motivational speakers. They tell us that we are wonderful, that our possibilities are limitless, and that if we will simply believe in ourselves we can accomplish anything. We are *not* wonderful in every way, we do not operate without certain limitations, and merely believing ourselves omnipotent will not make ourselves so.[19]

Most of these quick self-esteem programs are about as successful as the latest diet. They make all sorts of promises they cannot possibly deliver.

Yet within the Christian tradition there are powerful resources for supporting a healthy self-concept. The incomparable uniqueness of every person, the unconditional love of God, the belief that our individual lives can have personal meaning and the realization that we can make a contribution toward a better world are all excellent reasons to value ourselves. But the transforming element in our ability to respect ourselves is the capacity to give and receive love. Paul's words are an important daily reminder:

> If I speak in the tongues of mortals and of angels, but do not have love, I am a noisy gong or a clanging cymbal. And if I have prophetic powers, and understand all mysteries and all knowledge, and if I have all faith, so as to remove mountains, but do not have love, I am nothing. If I give away all my possessions, and if I hand over my body so that I may boast, but do not have love, I gain nothing. (1 Corinthians 13:1-3 NRSV)

We find our confidence not by frantically searching for it, but by instead throwing ourselves into the service of love. It is hard to like ourselves when we don't really respect ourselves. Nothing brings a greater sense of human fulfillment than employing our gifts in the service of expanding love. The ways in which we do this are quite individualized and unique to each of us. It may at times seem small, and it certainly doesn't have to be melodramatic. Yet as Frederick Buechner said so beautifully, "The place God calls you to is the place where your deep gladness and the world's deep hunger meet."[20]

4

RESPONDING WITH JUDGMENTS VS. REACTING WITH JUDGMENTALISM

If I were going to name the biggest daily challenge of life it would be *learning to respond rather than react.* When I'm reacting, I'm not working from my centeredness in grace. Instead, I'm allowing outside factors to control my behavior. And much of the time, my reaction is judgmental.

As a rule, judgmentalism does *react* rather than *respond.* Judgmentalism is almost always controlled by outside factors. When we become judgmental, we are often controlled by the very groups we fight. Outside enemies control our agenda. We can't leave them alone. They determine our thinking in that we *must* rail against them. We become far more able to tell others what we are *against,* rather than what we are *for.* We may feel pushed around and our paranoid defensiveness may snarl with yet another rebuke of something. We must condemn. Thus, we are not free to initiate, share or offer our perspective. We are compulsively driven to conquer anything that does not look like us!

THE ROOTS OF REACTIVITY

Cognitive therapist Aaron Beck offers some insight into how we become so reactionary.[1] As a cognitive psychiatrist, Beck believes that emotional disturbance results from distorted thinking. In other words, our tendencies to think in exaggerated, irrational ways set us up for unnecessary emotional distress. Our feelings follow our thoughts, and so if we want to heal our feelings, we should look at the underlying thought processes that have created them. So distorted thinking creates disturbed feelings. These disturbed feelings then push us into a reactionary mode. This is certainly not to suggest that feelings are bad, but it is to suggest that feelings are the results of prior acts of interpretation.

According to Beck, when we feel threatened, we often regress to a more "primitive" way of thinking. Beck believes that early in human history it was very important for us to quickly assess a situation and react with a snap judgment. This was essential to our survival. We had to determine whether someone was a friend or foe. Rapid thinkers survived; slower, calculating thinkers often did not. So in that world, making fast judgments born out of an "us" and "them" mentality was crucial. Being physically threatened necessitated this type of thinking.

The problem, however, is that we learned this way of surviving *too well*. In other words, even when we are not physically threatened, we easily fall back into this adaptive mode of thinking. In fact, when we feel emotionally or psychologically threatened, it is easy to revert to this primitive thinking process. The problem, of course, is that these psychological threats are of a completely different nature. We are not *really* in danger even though our minds tend to automatically prepare us for attack. Our higher-level thinking, which is located in the neocortex, is important for us to be able to consider options and think creatively in the face of differences and conflicts with others, but our primal thinking crowds out the possibility of engaging in this higher-order thinking.

Another aspect of reactive thinking is that it is highly egocentric. In other words, when we feel threatened we often become quite obsessed with ourselves and our own safety. While self-interest is important, in the face of threat we can become preoccupied with how *everything* affects us. All data is assessed quickly and egocentrically. Exaggerated thinking promotes excessive anxiety, which pushes us toward reactionary judgmentalism. We think in highly biased ways: we are righteous, and the other person is evil; we are the victims, and they are the victimizers; we are 100 percent innocent, and they are completely guilty; we must attack the enemy because they are trying to attack us.

In table 4.1, I have summarized the basic differences between responding and reacting. I encourage readers to examine their own patterns. If you are like me, you will find that you react far more often than you'd like.

Table 4.1. Responding vs. Reacting

Responding	Reacting
Responding comes from a centered self.	Reacting comes from being self-centered.
Responding respects another's boundaries.	Reacting wants to control others' lives.
Responding is able to distinguish thoughts and feelings.	Reacting lumps thoughts and emotions together.
Responding emerges from intentional reflection.	Reacting emerges from unreflective impulsivity.
Responding comes from a careful mind not controlled by emotion.	Reacting comes from thoughtless motivation controlled by feelings.
Responding results from an internal decision.	Reacting results from external triggers and internal compulsion.
Responding results from confident conviction.	Reacting results from shaky and threatened beliefs.
Responding recognizes the existence of alternative views.	Reacting insists that all views be like its own.
Responding sees the context of another's behavior.	Reacting defines personhood by a single act.

If I am responding, I will speak and act from a sense of centeredness: my actions will result from an inner sense of choice. I won't be provoked into action, "made" angry or "set off" by someone's remark. I will live in my own skin and be fully responsible for my actions. However, if I react I will normally be preoccupied with having the final word, telling someone off or making sure they know I'm right.

If I'm responding to others, I will respect their boundaries as I voice my concerns, offer suggestions or share my own experience. I will regularly remind myself that I'm not behind the steering wheel of their lives. When I'm reacting, though, I don't respect these boundaries; I attempt to manipulate, dominate or coerce them into my viewpoint.

When I'm responding, I can be aware of what I'm feeling but not necessarily allow those feelings to dictate my response. While I do not deny my feelings, neither am I utterly controlled by them. Again, my responses are deliberate and voluntary. When I'm reacting, on the other hand, my intense feelings are pushing my buttons and I lose control. I can't seem to separate my feelings from how I want to respond. I think emotionally. Thus, flooded with emotions, I act without much thinking. My behavior is involuntary and often exaggerated.

When I'm responding, my behavior results from internal decision and conviction. I am not controlled by external factors that make up my mind for me. I pause, consider and reflect. I refuse a knee-jerk reaction. Conversely, my reactivity emerges from external stress and pressure. I simply must attack. In reality, however, my reactivity is normally based on fairly shaky attitudes or beliefs.

When I'm responding, I recognize that many perspectives exist and that there is often more than one way to do things. I'm not afraid of alternative views. I will also look at the context of someone else's life. Then again, when I'm reactive, I'm often demanding that others think as I think and do everything my way. I may judge their entire being on the basis of one decision or act.

RESPONSE-ABLE ASSERTIVENESS VS. REACTIONARY AGGRESSION

If we hope to become less judgmental, it is essential that we work on our own levels of reactivity. And in order to improve our ability to be responsive, rather than reactive, it is important to understand our patterns of anger.

Clearly, many of us are uncomfortable with feelings of anger. We think anger is an ugly feeling. We may have seen unfortunate things happen when people got angry, so we've decided to not go there. We may have confused the *emotion* of anger with aggressive *behavior*. Therefore, anger has become a negative emotion, one we should live above. We may eat our anger, deny our irritations and sweep our frustrations under the rug of denial.

Also, we may believe that if we get angry, others may reject or abandon us. Because security is so important, we may not run the risk of being honest about even our persistent feelings of anger. Phoniness is the price we pay for this security. We may well become a doormat and a very nonassertive person. We may feel both an internal and external pressure to constantly please, win favor and be agreeable. This leads to conflict-phobia. Differences between ourselves and others are very threatening. We become preoccupied with nurturing our relationships at the expense of being genuine. The goal of maintaining harmony is turned into a god. We may maintain a reputation as an "easygoing Joe," a "patient professional" or a "never-angry representative of eternal kindness." We may confuse nurture with false comfort; humility with self-deprecation; being dependable with being used; being gentle with being a pushover. Lack of self-approval pushes us toward a frantic need for the approval of others. Our self-esteem is always in someone else's hands.

I also need to regularly remind myself that if I am not comfortable with my own anger, I will probably downplay, minimize or avoid someone else's anger. If I am phony and do not admit my anger, I may well invite others into a pretentiously sweet, anger-free relationship. I may indeed indirectly communicate that anger is off-limits, or that our relationship could not survive anyone getting angry.

Yet anger is very hard to permanently ignore. Perhaps what happens to the majority of us is that we keep storing our anger in the basement until one day we explode. The explosion is often an exaggeration because it is based on an accumulation of emotion. The buildup is so strong that we bypass assertiveness and move straight into aggression. By not addressing issues when they come up, we end up with a slush fund that demands a loud outburst. We've stockpiled the anger, and it is all coming out at once. We've tried to be too "nice" and now realize that we must pick up the tab. And unfortunately, after we have exploded we then feel guilty or embarrassed and decide once again that we simply should not get angry. This pushes us back into the passive-aggressive cycle in which we once again ignore our anger until the next explosion. We want desperately to avoid our anger, but we find that it inevitably builds up and ambushes us again.

Consider the number of times we let things slide and choose to say nothing even though we feel somewhat insulted. A student was telling me that she had listened to so many caricatures of Christianity in one of her classes, heard so many negative comments about "religious nuts" and "intolerant people" of faith that she let it all build up and one day blurted out that another student was "just a narrow-minded, idiotic atheist who didn't know anything." We both talked about how this comment was unfortunate, but we also saw how it had built up because of her lack of assertiveness. On many occasions, she could have questioned the evidence of the other student's belief or simply reported that her own experience had been different. She could have recognized that while there is a lot of distortion of healthy faith, this distortion doesn't tell the whole story. She may have even suggested that religion doesn't have a monopoly on intolerance. But she felt shy and wanted to be "nice." Yet the niceness caught up with her. The other student then smugly used this as an example of how religious people really are hostile. This other student was completely unaware of how her own hostile attitude helped provoke the reaction.

If we are going to become less reactionary and tell the truth in love, then we need to improve our ability to recognize and express our anger. Explosive anger and reactionary tendencies go hand in hand. But we need to be patient with our patterns of anger as we realize that they were not developed overnight. They cannot be instantly changed; instead, it takes some work. We need to examine what we saw modeled in our family of origin, because we may still be imitating those patterns or going to the opposite extreme and doing the complete reverse of what we saw modeled. Either way, we may be controlled by tendencies we are not really choosing freely. We need to sort out our parents' conflict issues from our own. This may even involve metaphorically giving back to our parents their unresolved anger issues, which belong to them and not to us. Some of us may realize, for instance, that we have been carrying for years our parents' unacknowledged and therefore unprocessed anger issues.

Also, shaming or judging our feelings of anger will not help us deal with them. We need to fully digest the realization that anger is natural, inevitable and, in itself, neutral. People who have no ability to get angry are missing a vital ingredient of being human. If we recognize this inevitability of anger, we may then be able to detect anger at an early stage and do something constructive with it. We must not let it snowball or else reactivity will surely follow.

Our reactivity will also be minimized when we can own our anger as *our* feeling instead of blaming others for having made us mad. Others' behavior may be intricately involved in our anger, but it is still our anger and we can choose what to do with it. We can better understand what triggers our anger (what types of personalities, situations, behaviors and attitudes set us off?), what patterns have *not* worked for us in sorting through our anger and what alternative strategies there are for dealing with anger. It is also helpful to talk about these personal struggles with trusted friends. Being aware of them, and regularly reminding ourselves that we are responsible for how we respond, may help us become less reactionary.

> If you test me and I take the anger bait, then it is still not you who are making me angry. For seeking to bait me, you are responsible. But it is I who choose, consciously or unconsciously, to take the anger bait; for that I am responsible. And if I continue to take the bait as often as you offer it, I am either refusing to learn from my experience or I am getting some rewards from my bait snatching.[2]

Further, without denying what we feel, it is also important to quickly ask ourselves if we may be overreacting to a situation. Are we interpreting an event or behavior in all-or-nothing, inflated or exaggerated ways? If so, what might this be telling us about our own fears and insecurities? This mental habit of "checking ourselves," without denying our feelings, is crucial. The greater awareness we have, the more options we have available. Reactivity does not see any options available; instead, it feels that it simply must attack. This time of deliberate pausing may help us understand when we need a time-out from a situation that is too intense. All of us have a point at which we can no longer be constructive in our expression of anger. Postponing a confrontation does not necessarily involve denying anger.

If we are approaching people about an issue, we need to drop the word *confrontation*. If we begin a conversation with someone by saying, "I need to confront you about something," the other person's guard will immediately go up and he or she may already feel attacked. The word puts most people on the defensive. So, it is more helpful to say that we'd like to mention a few things, suggest a few things, or share some of your thoughts and feelings. David Augsburger has created the very helpful word "care-frontation" to get at the heart of what this kind of honesty entails.

> Care-fronting has a unique view of conflict. Conflict is natural, normal, neutral, and sometimes even delightful. It can turn into painful or disastrous ends, but it doesn't need to. Conflict is neither good nor bad, right nor wrong. Conflict simply is. How we view, approach and work through our differences does—to a large extent—determine our whole life pattern.[3]

This approach will exclude name-calling, abusive labeling or other forms of mudslinging. It will not make threats of violence. It will also work hard to avoid generalizations: "You're always late," or "You're just lazy, stupid, irresponsible or immoral." *Never, always, totally, completely* and *absolutely* are not words that lead to interpersonal peace. Also, it's important to avoid trying to read someone else's mind. This can lead to enormous reactivity. Further, the other person may not even be thinking what we assume they are.

The discomfort we may first feel when we become assertive is worth it. Assertiveness promotes care for others; it does not cancel out that care. It is the anger-denying passivity, which eventually explodes, that is the real threat to caring for others. Far more damage to relationships is done by accumulated aggression than by honesty. Resentments are monstrous destroyers of interpersonal peace. They recycle old feelings, issues and experiences without voicing them. They eliminate being in the present and chain us to the past. They cultivate an inner picture of an enemy by whom we feel victimized until we explode. Resentments often tag along with superficial politeness. They keep us stuck in what someone else has done to us, rather than help us move toward our own choices and fulfillment.

We also frequently overreact to the behavior of others because we feel responsible for them. Overextending our sense of responsibility is a major source of frustration and anxiety. It propels us into the false belief that we ought to be able to control another. This reverses the serenity prayer and attempts to change things we cannot control while ignoring things we can change. And sometimes our reactivity toward others stems from the simple fact that we are not minding our own business, but instead are involved in running someone else's life.

Again, the choice is never between getting angry or not getting angry. The choice revolves around what to do with our anger when it arises. A great deal of reactivity results from repressed anger for which we feel ashamed. Having accumulated, it then explodes on a path of reactivity. We must become adept at recognizing and accepting our anger at early, manageable stages.

Becoming less judgmentally reactionary and more responsive is an ongoing, daily task in which we never "arrive." Yet as we continue to receive the grace of God and allow that grace to transform our relationships, we are freed to listen, care and respond more fully. As David Augsburger writes:

A context of caring must come before confrontation. A sense of support must be present before criticism. An experience of empathy must precede evaluation. A basis of trust must be laid before one risks advising. A floor of affirmation must undergird any assertiveness. A gift of understanding opens the way to disagreeing. An awareness of love sets us free to level with each other. Building solidarity in relationships with others—through caring, support, empathy, trust, affirmation, understanding and love—provides a foundation for the more powerful actions of confrontation, criticism, evaluation, counsel, assertiveness, disagreement and open leveling with each other.[4]

5

GUILTY JUDGMENTS VS. SHAMEFUL JUDGMENTALISM

Judgmentalism is often tied to an unhealthy sense of shame. When I say *unhealthy* shame, I am distinguishing this experience from the feelings of embarrassment or the awareness that I have violated the rights of others. If I rudely cut in line at the movie theater, it is appropriate for me to feel a healthy sense of shame; I have ignored my own limitations as well as the rights of others. Or if I do something highly embarrassing, it is appropriate for me to feel a temporary sense of shame. This is a passing feeling of sudden exposure, being caught off guard or looking silly. Yet unhealthy shame is a deep-rooted conviction that I am defective and worthless. It is exaggerated, self-indicting and destructive. Its aim is not to change my behavior; instead, its aim is ridicule and total condemnation.

Shame is connected to judgmentalism in two ways. First, when we are on the receiving end of judgmentalism, it is easy to fall prey to shame. Second, when we are being judgmental, we are often working very hard to cover our own shame by shaming others. Shame believes only in condemnation and not in grace. But shame is not simply a psychological problem. It can become a theological problem as well. If we hold an excessively shameful and judgmental view of ourselves, we will very often project that onto God. We will become convinced that God's attitude toward us is full of harsh contempt. When this happens, we are not just doing battle with our own inner critic, but instead we believe that God is as disgusted with us as we are with ourselves. The notion of grace cannot seem to get past our own self-condemnation.

Perhaps this was exactly the situation in which Martin Luther found himself when he was in the monastery. Full of self-loathing, Luther *knew* that God hated him as well. And Luther, as an astute depth-psychologist as well as a theologian, also knew that he could never consciously name all of his sins. When he thought he had confessed them all, others would surface. He felt trapped in a world of divine wrath. And Luther was willing to be profoundly honest: As he felt hated by God, he hated this God back. Constantly feeling condemned, he eventually admitted hating the condemner. It was precisely in this situation that Luther experienced the profound divine acceptance, which was able to both transform his image of God and help him think differently about himself. Shame was transformed by grace.

There is something sadly audacious when the very Ground and Source of our lives, the God of love, offers us acceptance and transforming love while we persist in our old condemning habits and insist that we stand unredeemable. This shame is an inverted form of grandiosity: we think we are too far gone, even for God's love.

Over the past few decades, a great deal of clinical interest has focused on the differences between the experiences of guilt and shame. For the purposes of the rest of this chapter, when I use the word *shame,* I am referring to the unhealthy form of the word. Guilt, which is a very important ingredient for a spiritually mature and emotionally healthy life, must be clearly distinguished and separated from shame. Again, it is important to separate these two experiences for this reason: *While guilt is the partner of judgment, shame is the mate of judgmentalism.* Even after they have been embraced by God's grace, some still need some help in distinguishing appropriate guilt and shame. Let's look at some key distinctions between the two.

DISTINGUISHING BETWEEN GUILT AND SHAME

If I were compiling a profile of guilt which has turned into shame, I would say that shame exaggerates and condemningly labels us; it attacks us with all-or-nothing thinking; it does *not* respond to forgiveness; it drives us into isolation and inverted grandiosity; it does *not* motivate change; it is tied to perfectionism; and it encourages self-punishment.

Conversely, limited healthy guilt invites us to turn a deaf ear to exaggerated self-talk; it looks at specific, concrete behavior and attitudes we want to change; it *does* respond to forgiveness; it encourages us to share mistakes with trusted friends; it motivates us to change; it is based on obtainable, realistic goals; and it sees the futility of self-punishment.

I've delineated these further in table 5.1 and describe them in detail below.

Shame exaggerates what we have done, blows things out of proportion and uses negative labels to describe *us* rather than our *behavior.* It resorts to name-calling (idiot, tramp, bum, wimp) and loves the language of condemnation. It goes for overkill. It is out of proportion to our actual behavior. Healthy guilt, on the other hand, is specific about what we have done. Guilt might tell me that I was not very sensitive to a student's needs; shame would tell me that I don't care about my students at all. Guilt might tell someone that she neglected her daughter; shame would tell her that she is a lousy parent.

Shame attacks us with all-or-nothing thinking and global general-

Table 5.1. Differences Between Guilt and Shame

Guilt	Shame
Healthy guilt is specific about negative *actions* taken, rather than labeling *itself*.	Shame exaggerates what it has done, labeling *itself* negatively, rather than its *behavior.*
Healthy guilt focuses on specific things to change and resists clobbering with a totalistic judgment.	Shame attacks with all-or-nothing thinking and global generalizations.
Healthy guilt opens the path to self-forgiveness and is encouraged to accept its frailties. It sees the worthwhile person underneath the unhealthy behavior.	Shame does not respond to forgiveness.
Guilt involves the sharing of failure and regret with trusted friends.	Shame drives itself into isolation, loneliness and feelings of unique depravity. It hides from others and itself.
Healthy guilt stays with the modest agenda of looking for specific change, without threatening its own worth.	Shame does *not* motivate toward constructive change; it immobilizes in inactivity.
Healthy guilt lets go of grandiosity and unrealistic standards.	Shame is often linked to an ideal standard.
Healthy guilt sees the pointlessness of self-punishment and understands that it is a block to self-acceptance. It makes amends and leaves it at that.	Shame encourages some form of self-punishment in an irrational attempt to "atone" for what has happened.

izations. It says that we or someone else is "completely irresponsible," "absolutely worthless" or "just a bum." Again, notice that these messages never provide specific information we can use. Instead, they leave us feeling helpless, hopeless and impaled by the condemnation. Healthy guilt, on the other hand, recognizes—during calmer, more rational moments—that these pronouncements are ridiculous and unfair. They are based on dualistic thinking, which provides us with no help for change. Healthy guilt focuses on specific things we can change and resists clobbering us with a totalistic judgment. Guilt is more modest, more focused, more concerned with our recovery from the fault than simply blasting the fault.

Shame does not respond to forgiveness. It puts us on a cycle of compulsive, perpetual confessing, but it offers no sense of relief. We constantly say we're sorry, and sometimes we don't even know why we're saying it. No amount of apologizing seems to bring inner peace. Healthy guilt, however, opens the path to self-forgiveness and encourages us to accept our frailties. We can allow ourselves to be released from the irresponsibilities of our pasts and face our futures without the dead weight of our former mistakes. Healthy guilt allows us to embrace and own our pasts while keeping our self-worth intact. It realizes that we cannot like ourselves today if we do not accept who we were yesterday. Healthy guilt always sees the worthwhile person underneath the destructive, or at least unhealthy, behavior.

Shame is the condition of Judas, a hopeless condition of self-condemnation. Shame drives us into isolation, loneliness and feelings of unique depravity. In addition to hiding from others, we often hide from ourselves. There is no redemption, only a psychological hell. Self-avoidance becomes essential if we are to dodge these inward persecutions. Christian theologian Dietrich Bonhoeffer states this very well:

> In confession the break-through to community takes place. Sin demands to have a man by himself. It withdraws him from the community. The more isolated a person is, the more destructive will be the power of sin over him, and the more deeply he becomes involved in it, the more disastrous in his isolation. Sin wants to remain unknown. It shuns the light. In the darkness of the unexpressed it poisons the whole being of a pious community.[1]

Guilt, on the other hand, is the condition of Peter, who betrayed Jesus and yet did not destroy himself. Guilt involves the sharing of failure and regret with trusted friends. It recognizes the power of allowing ourselves to be known and accepted. It acknowledges the deep need within each of us to reveal who we really are and open the door for support and acceptance. And it understands that God's love surpasses our heaviest condemnation.

Shame does *not* motivate us toward constructive change or encourage us to make amends. It never provides us with a vision of how to do these things. Instead, it freezes and immobilizes us in a morbid world of inactivity, leaving us feeling stuck. Healthy guilt, on the other hand, moves us toward change, growth and the building of better lives. We feel motivated rather than devastated. Why? Because healthy guilt stays with the modest agenda of looking for specific change. Our self-awareness is an educational tool: we do not have to feel threatened as we look at ourselves; our worth is not being challenged.

Shame is often linked to perfectionism or an ideal standard. These unrealistic demands make failure inevitable. Shame is fueled by impossible expectations, ruthless standards that often leave us in one of two predicaments. First, we may feel exhausted, defeated and depressed. Second, we may angrily rebel against these dictates, revolting against ourselves in a self-defeating protest. We may spend most of our time trying to get out from under these rigid, demeaning voices, yet even when we rebel against them, these standards *are still controlling us.* We are fighting ourselves, and the battle takes all our energy. Either way, whether we follow or fight our perfection, it leaves us empty and condemned. Healthy guilt, on the other hand, allows us to let go of our grandiosity and unrealistic standards. We can deflate our perfectionism, and seek realistic, human, obtainable goals. While we need not shortchange our potential, we can embrace our limitations and learn to live with them. Not having to be perfect can relieve us of unnecessary anxiety.

Shame encourages some form of self-punishment in an irrational attempt to "atone" for what has happened or what we have done.

Shame puts us on a roller coaster of trying to compensate for our feelings of failure. We may constantly tell people that we will "make it up to them," and then take on impossible tasks to alleviate our feelings of shame. We may completely overextend ourselves in doing things for a friend we think we've neglected. We may punish our bodies by abstaining from food after we've overeaten. Healthy guilt, however, sees the futility of self-punishment and understands that it is a block to self-acceptance. Once amends are made, the issue is dropped. The point is to change, not make up for the past.

Grace vs. shame and guiltlessness vs. justice. Healthy guilt is undergirded and insured by Jesus' grace. Like a person walking a tightrope, we have a safety net of acceptance available to us. Sadly, many of us do not accept or rely on this. We act or believe as if wrong moves are fatal. But our *being* is not on trial anymore. We are not synonymous with our behavior. We can rest easy. The stakes are not that high. We don't have to panic. In fact, we can review our behavior and use this core sense of acceptance to generate change.

Grace, God's unconditional prizing we find in the midst of our critical investigations, is transforming. We do not need to change in order to gain acceptance. Acceptance is there free for the taking. What we do with that acceptance is a response of gratitude. We can never do enough to get out of the shame pit, but we can, as Paul Tillich frequently said, "accept our acceptance." At that point we will have a foundation on which to build.

I remember reading, from an author I unfortunately cannot recall, that guilt, when it is functioning in a healthy manner, is somewhat similar to an alarm clock. Even though most of us do not like the sound of an alarm clock when it goes off in the morning, the alarm serves a very important function—namely, alerting us to the time of day. The clock wakes us up to a decision: Do we get up or do we remain in bed? While it may seem that we have no choice, we actually do, especially if we are willing to pay the consequences of not getting up. The alarm needs to be loud enough to wake us up, but not so loud that it impairs our hearing. Further, we need to be able to turn it off. An alarm clock we could not turn off would merely be dead noise we carry around all day. Both the duration and the intensity of the alarm need to be limited.

Similarly, guilt simply alarms us about a decision we need to make. There is a discrepancy between our values and our behavior. This inconsistency needs to be addressed. For instance, my beliefs or values may tell me that I should treat others as I would like to be treated. Guilt may remind me that I was quite insensitive to someone yesterday. I, therefore, need to apologize to that person and work toward not doing that again. After I have acknowledged my fault and made amends, it becomes fruitless to allow guilt to continue to sabotage my mental peace—this would be like the alarm clock that could not be turned off.

Yet at other times, the split between my beliefs and my behavior may reveal that my *beliefs,* rather than my *behavior,* need to be changed. For example, I may have an absolutely essential meeting at work at the same time that a close friend is in a play. I may feel guilty because I cannot be at both places at the same time. In such a situation, it is perhaps my unrealistic belief system that needs to be changed. I may feel *sad* that I cannot attend the play, but there is no reason to feel guilty. As Thomas Oden suggests, this is simply the human plight: Choosing one value sometimes means negating another.[2] It would be nice if we lived in a world in which there was only one good choice and all the others were negative, but that is not the way life operates.

Because guilt is often an uncomfortable experience, some have reacted to guilt in one of two extreme ways. One way, which has been unfortunately fueled by some schools of psychotherapy, is to consider *all* guilt as neurotic and unhelpful. This view often leads to reckless abandonment of guilt. Guilt is pointless and gets in the way of one's own fulfillment. Oden describes his reaction to this type of guiltless attitude about using abortion as a means of birth control:

> Indelibly imprinted on my mind is the strained face of a fifteen-year-old girl in a television interview. With two abortions already, she was soon to have a third. Asked what she had against contraceptives, she shrugged with shocking simplicity: "Sex just feels better without them," which meant that abortion had heedlessly and blatantly become a means of birth control. . . . That portion of the interview was shocking enough: to realize that human life, God's first and greatest gift, is being bartered off thoughtlessly for the momentary élan of sexual pleasure. But the sequel was even more shocking. An "eminent psychiatrist" was then brought in to talk to the teenager and television audience about guilt that emerges out of consideration of abortion. He approved of her low guilt awareness as healthy and suggested that if she worried too much about the morality of her action, it would further complicate her life. I have never quite gotten over that five-minute interview, and what it implies for our society.[3]

Indeed, this type of utter disregard for responsible guilt scares many of us. By assuming that all feelings of obligation, duty and moral responsibility are simply the hangovers of a repressive conscience, some individuals have distorted the notion of self-actualization into a hedonistic form of self-indulgence. Again, some psychotherapies in the sixties and seventies, especially, sought to liberate people from all the pangs of conscience. Because some had been troubled by an overactive conscience in the past, it was believed that the solution was to rid themselves of all prohibitory, restrictive and restraining voices. While Freud is sometimes blamed for some of these psychotherapeutic tendencies, it is important to note that the later Freud believed that without some degree of social restraint and responsibility, human nature would move toward destruction. Freud was much more sober about the overthrow of conscience than were many of his followers.

Another major factor in the overthrow of guilt was the growing belief that destructive human behavior always comes from outside factors and not from responsible choice. For example, there is always an external cause for "sin," and we should never look toward human volition as part of evil.

Judges hearing criminal cases have often viewed guilt not as a real offense against society, but only as an ambiguous result of social and economic deprivation, determined by outward circumstances rather than any responsible acts of will. On this basis, they have left victims unprotected and have promptly pardoned offenders allowing them to return to mug, plunder, and rape again. Ironically, these judges have dishonored the self-respect of our anti-social citizens by assuming they have no self-determining wills. . . . Recent theology has colluded with the modern idea that guilt is not real, and that it has obvious political, economic, and psychological remedies. Theology, too, has reduced the problem of guilt to social mechanics, political tinkering, and psychological determinism, and thereby withheld its unique gift at a time when society needed it most. Theology has in fact intensified this false hope of a quick fix with its own antinomian (lawless) version of the gospel: God's mercy without human social effort, pardon without requirement, grace without covenant accountability, God's unconditional love without any mention of justice.[4]

Guilt is very often reduced to mere guilt *feelings*. This psychological captivity of an ethical issue does not allow for a genuine release from real guilt, the violation of ethical standards important to individuals and their communities. It is very important to realize that our sense of brokenness, guilt and "falling short" of God's intention for our lives doesn't simply emerge from a fictional idea or the internalization of an external reality. It emerges because we know, at a deep level, that we are not living consistently with our own deepest desires for a life of love and justice.

While many conservative Christians have been very alert to this social sense of "guiltlessness," they have often not paid enough attention to excessive guilt problems in their own congregations. In other words, just as guilt has been thrown out in some circles, it has also been exaggerated in others. Many individuals have struggled mightily to get out from under the feelings of neurotic guilt and abusive conceptions of themselves. Some Christians have wrestled with these feelings of excessive guilt, or what I would prefer calling shame. Because the entire concept of self-esteem has been treated with great suspicion, and such a strong emphasis has been placed on pride, arrogance and self-exaltation, some have concentrated on their "depraved" nature at the expense of seeing anything positive about themselves. "Total depravity" has been understood to imply that we could not possibly be any worse than we are. Just as Augustine went to the extreme with the Pelagians of arguing that unbaptized babies will be damned, so the Reformers, and especially Calvin, attempted to block any notion of works righteousness with an overstated view of human depravity. And perhaps we should be honest about part of the "guiltless predicament" we have inherited: Part of it is a reaction to the excessive guilt of previous generations, a guilt fixated on ethical trivia, an oppressive conscience, and the assumption that an enjoyable life and a faithful life are mutually exclusive. Perhaps an example would help. I know a church that split up because a pool table was placed in the recreation center for the youth. That's right, the church split because of this "highly serious" moral issue. While most of us would be concerned that kids are snorting cocaine off this pool table, this particular church was fixated on playing pool. Even when there was no betting on the outcome of the game, pool was too much.

Now, granted, this is an extreme case. But some evangelicals have not paid adequate attention to the self-disdain, self-contempt and sense of shame in the psyches of many conservatives. As I talked about in an earlier chapter, even evangelical scholars have often been quick to support the "primacy of pride and self-exaltation" position because it matches their Calvinistic roots. But I would like to also suggest that shame may have many ways of hiding its face. It can work behind the scenes even in behavior that does not explicitly look like shame. Consider these examples.

- A need to dominate and control others may stem from our own suspicion that we're not strong enough.

- Disregard and disrespect for others may emerge from our inability to be compassionate with ourselves.

- Adoration of power may come from our own sense of powerlessness.

- Proud perfectionism may emerge from our fear of self-beatings if our flaws are discovered.

- Relentless competition may result from our fear of losing all worth if we're not the best.

- A need to be intellectually superior may emerge from our fear of appearing stupid or uncertain.

- Detached aloofness may come from a deep fear of needing others.

- Sarcasm about new projects or activities may be connected to a fear of failing at new tasks.

- Preoccupation with ourselves may be triggered by worry as to how we are coming across.

- A negative, belittling attitude toward anyone ambitious may stem from our own fear of hoping, expanding or wanting "too much."

- Disdain for other people and their foul motives may come from a deeper worry about our own gullibility and potential victimization.

- Distrust of relationships and fear of commitment may be related to our own distrust in our own powers of discrimination.

- A clinging, smothering, boundary-violating suffocation may be triggered by discomfort with aloneness and abandonment anxiety.

- A craving for attention and praise may emerge from a lack of self-respect and confidence.

- An excessive need for affection may well be related to a lack of self-appreciation.

- A tendency to dodge stress and run away from problems may be connected to anxiety about our inner strength.

- An inclination to complain, whine and be miserable may come from a fear of giving up a victim status.

Beneath each of these behaviors lurks a shame issue. We try to make the shame go away by proving that we are not what the shame is whispering to us.

If we want to help people with shame and judgmentalism, we must see beneath the surface and understand what may be going on beneath. Stated differently, not all self-elevation should be taken at face value. It may be present and, at times, be very difficult to endure. But it is often driven by a more basic sense of inadequacy. Why *does* anyone need to regularly brag if they have solid self-confidence? Why *does* anyone need to constantly highlight themselves if they feel secure inside? Beneath these boisterous displays, I would suggest, is an injured self with much shame. And the sad reality is that the more frantically the shame is covered up, the more of a grip it holds.

SHAME AS JUDGMENTALISM TURNED INWARD

Anyone who has spent much time with people in counseling understands how a sense of shame can speak through an internalized, critical voice of condemnation. We may not beat ourselves physically, but we brutalize ourselves mentally. How? By exaggerated criticisms, condemnations, self-judgments and generalizations. We magnify our flaws and completely blow things out of proportion. We start an avalanche of verbal self-abuse. We may not talk out loud when this is going on, but the battering still occurs subvocally. A snickering, heckling, demeaning voice comments on our shortcomings. Judgmentalism is active. Mistakes are interpreted as failures. Being uninformed is labeled as "stupid." This condemning voice loves the hype of emotionally-charged language. It is a master at name-calling. In short, it turns us into our own worst enemy. Self-judgmentalism is precisely that—*self*-judgment. It is not judgment of specific behaviors or traits. Instead it is condemnation of the entire *self*.

Here's an example from my own life. I remember leaving class feeling disappointed that there had not been more discussion that evening. As the last few minutes of the class set in, I had thought to myself, *They are not interested in this material at all!* As I left the school and walked to my car, I began to think that the entire class must not be going very well. After I had gotten in my car and was driving home, my negative, exaggerated thoughts continued: *I've failed in this class. Perhaps I'm boring.* As I approached my home I was thinking, *You know, maybe I'm just not a very good teacher.* This was followed quickly by, *Perhaps I never should have gone into education.* And finally, *I'm a failure.* Again, these thoughts happened very rapidly. By the time I was getting ready for bed, I was frustrated and depressed.

When my class met again the next time, I asked them to give me some anonymous feedback. I asked them to address the issue of class discussion. When I reviewed the evaluations, there was nothing negative whatsoever. In fact, many of the students apologized for being so tired during the prior session and for not saying much. They went on to say that they didn't ask a lot of questions because everything seemed very clear to them.

My self-judgmentalism had pushed me into very negative feelings about my teaching. I had exaggerated, distorted and magnified what was going on in the previous class. I read into their fatigue a complete boredom with what I was saying. *Their* lack of discussion must mean that *I* am a lousy instructor. This episode reminded me of how important it is to check things out before beginning a process of self-judgmentalism. As I thought about it, I realized that I had done nothing differently the week before from what I normally do. And I also realized that this lack of discussion had been an exception to the rule. The students normally talked a great deal about issues. Yet that hypercritical voice in my own head wouldn't allow me to see this. And I have talked with several other professors who have told me that they also do this more often than they'd like to admit.

A self-judgmentalist mentality is a grace-resistant, antagonistic, demeaning internal enemy. It can ambush us, indict us and keep us frozen in unhealthy attitudes and behavior. Common messages sound like this: *I'm unattractive. I'm stupid. I'm not well liked. I'm never even noticed. I'm too emotional. I must be boring. I'm inadequate. I'm inferior. I'm too insecure. I have no confidence. I'm ashamed of myself. I don't know how to have any fun. I'm too shy. I'm self-centered. I'm irresponsible. I'm immature. I'm just a coward. I'm lazy. I've failed in all my relationships. I can't take criticism. I don't make enough money. What if I'm wrong? What will they think of me? I'll never fit in. I could never work there. I could never learn that. I can't change. I'm a psychological mess. I'm a weak person. No one can get along with me. I'm completely disorganized. I'm not lovable. I'm hopeless.*

These negative messages hound, heckle and distort our clear thinking about ourselves. Their function is to condemn, not to inform. Their task is wrecking self-confidence and keeping us within narrow restraints.

Again, notice the difference between making judgments and being judgmentalist. These internal statements attack *us* rather than our *behavior.* These fiery indictments are thrown at our being, our identity, our sense of worth. Judgmentalism is uninterested in the modest task of pointing toward specific behavior that could be changed. That's not dramatic enough. That's too limited in scope. Judgmentalism is hungry for an assault. Why concentrate on a specific habit or behavior when it can rage against the entire self! Why pass up a chance to be judgmental?

Judgmentalism's strategy is the "oversimplify and insult plan." We divide the world into all-or-nothing categories, then place ourselves in the negative group. We are either good or bad, compassionate or unfeeling, warm or cold, genuine or phony, hardworking or lazy, intelligent or stupid. Having made these tidy polar opposites, we then slam ourselves into the unattractive category. Again, much of this may occur at an unconscious level. As cognitive therapists often say, these are "automatic thoughts."

During rational moments, most of us recognize that we may not fit into this all-or-nothing classification scheme. We know that life is more complicated than that. We also recognize that we are somewhat different in every situation. It is unrealistic to say we are *always, completely, totally, absolutely, simply* or *just* anything. We're too complex for that.

Some of us have collected a highly judgmental series of images or pictures of ourselves, which we can pull out in our worst moments. This is a warehouse of negative, shaming, critical messages over the years. All the condemning voices from the outside now have an inside representative. A raging parent, for instance, no longer has to be present. We have taken over the job and learned to rage at ourselves. A humiliating teacher no longer has to suggest that we are stupid. We are happy to replay the old tape with a new level of intensity.

THREE WAYS WE DISGUISE OUR SELF-JUDGMENTALISMS

If I am walking down the street and I ask people how they are doing, they usually do not respond by saying, "Well, other than being excessively self-judgmental, shame-based and feeling inadequate, I'm doing fine." In fact, when we are struggling with self-judgmentalism, we usually find ways to camouflage it. We present a "compensatory self," an image designed to hide deeper feelings of self-contempt. There are three primary ways we attempt to dodge or detour around our self-judgmentalism. Karen Horney argued rather convincingly that, in the face of anxiety, we often develop one of these three interpersonal movements or trends that attempt to alleviate our insecurity.[5]

Toward others. The first movement is *toward* others. This typically involves an accommodating, self-sacrificing stance, which usually necessitates not paying much attention to ourselves as we try to please others. This trend is conflict-avoidant, even if that means that our own needs get ignored. The solution to potential conflict with another is simply to make sure we agree with the other person. Moving toward others, in Horney's scheme, means ignoring our own needs. In fact, there can be shades of masochism in this approach.

One of the most obvious cover-ups for self-doubt is approval-seeking. We seek, as a way of life, other people's endorsement, approval and validation. What others think becomes the guiding force in our lives. Our constant concern is how our behavior will affect someone else. We do things that will be pleasing, voice opinions in agreement with others and stay within the boundaries of someone's favor. We'll out-please the voice of self-judgmentalism. Surely this will keep our self-contempt at bay. Thus, our lives will not be lived from the *inside out;* instead, they'll flow from the *outside in.* We'll read and evaluate our performance from other people's faces, comments and reactions. Our self-esteem will be in their hands. Naturally, this will create enormous anxiety. After all, our acceptability will be continuously in front of an examining board. Their opinions matter, ours do not; their feelings are significant, ours are irrelevant; their perception of us must be accurate, while we know little of ourselves.

This approval-seeking puts us in a most precarious position. The sad fact is that we easily abandon ourselves as we focus on outside reactions. Other people dispense approval to us, and we seek it like starved creatures. We elevate their opinion to a godlike status and painfully ignore our own.

When we constantly seek approval from others we assume that

someone else's opinion is better simply because it is someone else's. Because nothing inside of us counts, we must find something outside of us for validation. Consequently, we believe we cannot depend on ourselves for an accurate picture of who we are. Others must have some secret information or inside dope on us. We are untrustworthy interpreters of our own experience. Eagerly, we look to others to tell us what we mean, what we've experienced and what we're all about. Unfortunately, there are plenty of people quite ready to offer their expert advice on *our* lives. These outsiders may never have felt our feelings, understood our past, nor appreciated the struggles of our experience. Yet we allow them to tell us what we should do and ought to have done. Further, we give them power to decide the way we see ourselves. Their opinion defines us. Our hunger for outside confirmation sets us up to be under their authority. This may seem really exaggerated, but I have seen some approval-seekers who are very much like this.

Eventually, however, most of us approval-seekers run out of steam. We become depressed, lose energy and sometimes feel like giving up. Life becomes an obligation, a burden, a curse. It is only when we start becoming aware of our pattern of self-avoidance that we can begin to regain strength. The unique individuals we are have often been neglected and abandoned long ago. We may have much sadness and anger about selling ourselves out. In fact, we may become outraged about the number of people we have put on a pedestal as more important than we are. We may begin to notice a long pattern of approval-seeking. We may discover that caring for others should not exclude taking care of ourselves. In fact, we may realize that self-care is essential if we are to have anything to give others. We may start to seek out friends with whom we can be ourselves, mutual friends who give as well as take. In fact, we may feel more inclined to let other people handle many of their own conflicts and not feel that our entire worth depends on solving everyone's problems. Recognizing our inability to control what anyone thinks about us can be a liberating experience. All that energy we poured into approval-seeking can be available for other pursuits.

Chronic approval-seeking will also leave us indecisive. There are many conflicting people to please. When we cannot count on ourselves for direction, we go through inner turmoil, frustration and confusion as we listen to others. Because there are so many voices, we often wander aimlessly trying to decide which one to follow. Many people will have opinions about what kind of car we should buy, whom we should date, where we should attend church, where we should go to school or how we should spend our day. Opinions are abundant and, without trust in ourselves, overwhelming. Careful thinking and consideration of outside opinions are one thing; attempting to please every advice-happy person we know is quite another. Indecisiveness often results from lack of confidence in our ability to handle a confusing situation, face a stress and choose for ourselves.

Related to this, when we desperately need the approval of others, we set ourselves up for being manipulated by them. When we need others' approval, they have power over us. This power can be used against us. They may withhold affection, make demands, invade our privacy or put us down. Because we need their approval so badly, we do not challenge or confront them. They have the "fix" we need, so the relationship is already out of balance. They have a secret weapon available—our neediness. We simply need their approval too much to be honest.

Changing our approval-seeking habits takes practice. We may have significant insights into our approval-seeking, understanding how we became this way and recognizing what this interpersonal habit has cost us. The solution to our problem, however, is in practicing a different way of life. Each time we face disapproval and maintain integrity, we gain inner confidence and strength. This is something we must *do*, not just something we think or feel. A change in behavior then reinforces our thinking, and we recognize the futility of chasing what we don't need. Until the time we do this, we may know it in our heads, but it has not yet become a gut-level reality.

It is important for us to fully see that chasing someone's approval can actually be a form of idolatry. No human being should be our god. The relentless pursuit of people's acceptance involves treating them as if they are divine. While this approval may be nice, it is not pivotal for our existence.

All change begins with awareness and assessment. Where has our approval-seeking gotten us? Well liked? Sometimes. Respected? Probably not. Most likely, others will not respect us until we respect ourselves. And all self-respect begins with paying attention. But paying attention to whom? Ourselves. This does not mean cosmetic attention, and it does not mean let's-impress-others attention. Instead, we offer ourselves a peaceful, private attention that encourages growth. It means noticing what we like, dislike, think, hope, dread and hate. This is the first step toward self-respect. We can learn to await, like expectant parents, what emerges within us. We don't have to avoid the voice of self-condemnation by pleasing everyone. In fact, we don't have the energy for it.

Against others. Horney's second interpersonal trend is moving *against* others. Out of our anxiety about differences, we attempt to dominate and control others. Threatened by these differences, we feel as if we must somehow conquer another person. We are not comfortable enough with ourselves to simply allow them to be who they are.

Instead, we must turn them into a clone of ourselves. If the first movement *toward* others involves possible masochism, this second movement *against* others may well involve sadism. It tends to drain the life out of another person because any type of liveliness is too threatening.

Judging, blaming and harshly criticizing others appears to have little to do with low self-esteem or a lack of self-acceptance. After all, judgmental and critical people are often loud, overbearing, dominating, arrogant and abusive. They do not look at all like the insecure approval-seekers I just discussed. Instead, they appear to be *too* self-assured, always right and never to blame. They have a built-in ability to excuse themselves from all mistakes and a keen ability to find fault outside themselves.

When we cannot admit mistakes and accept our human errors, we feel psychological pressure to locate all faults outside of ourselves. Any internal problem must be externalized. Of necessity, we must explain our problems on the basis of other people's behavior. Perpetual excuses are made to keep our image pure. It's *their* fault. *They* are to blame. Some villain outside of us is at work again. Blaming becomes the backbone of our refusal to emotionally grow up and be responsible for our lives.

It is very frightening to drop our blaming mask and look in the mirror. What will we find? Will we survive the inventory? Can we admit our mistakes without feeling *defined* by those mistakes? A shaky, fragile self-image will be too scared to explore very far. Living under the threat of excessive judgment pushes us to the outer world. The fault must be found *out there* because it is too painful to locate it *in here*. Blaming is thus a primary way of running away from ourselves. When we're blaming others, we are actually eliminating the possibility of self-knowledge. Firing away at the enemy out there keeps us away from inward discoveries. We actually need these culprits to escape ourselves. What would we do with no one to blame?

Blaming, then, is a stubborn block to self-ownership. We must recognize, admit and accept shortcomings as our own if we are to move beyond them. Any person or group that encourages blaming, either directly or indirectly, is an obstacle to healthy living. When we blame others, we sink deeper into a victim role. Blaming is born out of weakness, not strength. It has no vision, no hope, no motivation. It is giving up. It is allowing the power in our lives to be somewhere other than within us.

Blaming also poisons our relationships. Balance, fairness, perspective-taking, negotiating and responsibility are wiped out in a blizzard of critical accusations. It's always someone else who creates our mood, causes our behavior, makes us react, hurts our feelings, ruins our day or upsets us. We assume a passive, victim status and claim that others have contaminated, controlled and disabled us. How awful they are!

Recognizing our mistakes actually brings a liberating and relaxing willingness to be human. We can use our energies in productive ways rather than avoid self-contempt. The question is this: Do we use our psychological energies to protect, defend and stubbornly maintain our false self, or do we use those energies to explore, understand and improve ourselves? Is our posture primarily open or antagonistic? Fear of exposure can easily shut the door on self-discovery.

Judging, evaluating, assessing and analyzing others functions as a drug for many of us. It becomes the fix we need to escape our inner lives. By obsessing on the depravity of others, we distract our attention, gain a euphoric buzz of superiority and experience an adrenalin rush from policing someone else's behavior. Gossiping and criticizing become more and more necessary as we continue to avoid self-reflection. Once again, the simple rule is this: When we're judging others, we're avoiding ourselves. We can forget about what *we* need to change, how *we* are lacking and how *we* contribute to problems. Our accusations against others temporarily release us. We alter our moods by dissecting and ridiculing others. Deep within, our ongoing suspicion of inadequacy must be relieved through blaming someone. Yet the painful reality is this: No amount of external judgmentalism will heal our internal need for grace.

So once again, judgment of others is often a form of self-disgust. Others pick up the tab for our refusal to embrace, accept and become familiar with our own feelings of inadequacy. The battle within gets pushed outward. The enemy becomes projected so that we can crusade against what we secretly hate in ourselves. Others are manipulated into scapegoat carriers of our own shame. We rail against them, denounce them and proudly wonder how they became so vile. They are the targets of our own self-contempt.

It's very helpful to begin monitoring our blaming and judging patterns. We need not berate ourselves because of them. Then we'll have two problems: our judging habits and our judgmentalism *about* those judging habits! Instead, we can more gently ask ourselves what we may be dodging or avoiding through our judgmental mentality. Again, the way out of judgment is compassion, not more judgment. And this process requires ongoing divine support. We must recognize both God's love *for* us and God's love *in* us.

Away from others. Horney's third movement is *away* from others. This interpersonal trend involves compulsive isolation and disengagement from others. It attempts to solve the problem of anxiety and insecurity by a lifestyle of noninvolvement. It prefers detachment. Interpersonal involvement, it believes, tends to be messy and runs the risk of engulfment. The sense of self is not strong enough to risk any form of intimacy. It is far less threatening to remain unknown by anyone.

Sometimes we can attempt to escape our own self-judgmentalism by trying to appear detached, aloof, or too cool to be insecure. We may claim some form of invulnerability beyond what is humanly possible. Unconfident in our ability to get close to anyone, we may try to eliminate our need for human contact and appear quite self-sufficient. Our world remains carefully guarded. Self-disclosure is perceived as weakness and, hence, off-limits. Under all circumstances, we must remain calm, collected and unemotional. We must convince ourselves that we simply don't *need* anyone. Further, people who *do need* others are weak. In order to hide our self-judgmentalism we must remain unexposed. Intimate relationships have a way of exposing us not only to others but to ourselves as well. We certainly don't need that. Thus, in order to dodge ourselves, we must compulsively keep all matters on the surface. Introspection is a dangerous thing. Shallowness is essential to escape self-judgmentalism.

God's grace allows us to invest fully in this world even though we know life will break our hearts. C. S. Lewis once wrote: "Love anything and your heart will certainly be wrung and possibly be broken. If you want to make sure of keeping it intact, you must give your heart to no one, not even to an animal. . . . The only place outside Heaven where you can be perfectly safe from all the dangers and perturbations of love is Hell."[6] The adventure of loving, caring and throwing ourselves into the world is still worth it. Fear of involvement is based on a deeper insecurity that we could never survive disappointment. As Reinhold Niebuhr put it, "Faith in the providence of God is a necessity of freedom because, without it, the anxiety of freedom tempts man to seek a self-sufficiency and self-mastery incompatible with his dependence on forces which he does not control."[7] God's grace allows us to fully love because we have been loved.

I can only experience the freedom to love if I understand myself to be loved. The capacity to love is the gift of being loved. Love exists only as a response to being loved. I cannot love out of the poverty of my lovelessness. I cannot love merely in response to the idea of being loved, but only to the event, the reality of actually being loved.[8]

6

AUTHORITATIVE JUDGMENTS VS. AUTHORITARIAN JUDGMENTALISM

There is a huge difference between people who speak with *authority* and *authoritarians*. Authorities have knowledge, expertise and competence. Authoritarians, on the other hand, demand to be followed on the basis of sheer power, status and decree. Authorities do not feel personally attacked when we ask questions. Authoritarians insist on unquestioned loyalty even when they do not make sense. Whereas authorities exemplify rationality and wisdom, authoritarians demonstrate only power and control. As Howard Clinebell puts it:

> All of us need rational authority, the authority of competence. This was the authority with which Jesus spoke. His competence in spiritual matters was self-evident. His grasp of truth was unmistakably authentic.[1]

The word *authoritarian* refers to a pattern of thinking, a perspective on life, or a way of perceiving the world. Authoritarian thinking involves a rigid mentality. While the *content* of authoritarian thinkers may differ, the underlying *pattern* or *type* of reasoning is largely identical. In fact, authoritarianism and judgmentalism normally coexist. No group has a monopoly on it. Authoritarians can emerge from the right or the left. And regardless of its persuasion, authoritarian thinking is so *sure* it owns the truth that it feels justified in clobbering other people with it. Conversations are turned into power struggles in which we must conquer opposing viewpoints. Authoritarianism reveals an obsessive-compulsive mindset, an anxiety-ridden defensive mentality. Thus, authoritarianism must be seen as a dishonest attempt to manage the frightening anxiety inherent in life, an anxiety that must be faced by every person. Authoritarian thinking wants to be rescued from the dilemmas of humanity. It doesn't want to *trust;* it demands to *know.* And even if it does not know, it *pretends* it does. It is a mentality with great discomfort over the realities of daily life. In an effort to cope, it retreats into a cave of certainty and attacks all who come near.

Authoritarian thinking, by forcing all our experiences to fit into prearranged mental categories, plunges us into emotional disturbance. When we impose inadequate interpretations on our experience it is like walking around in shoes that are much too small for us: we will get blisters and have problems with our feet. We cannot consistently repress, avoid and unconsciously attempt to stamp out our experience without it eventually catching up with us. Clearly, there is a connection between denying life experiences and psychological dysfunction. Rigid thinking produces a highly restrictive emotional life, a psychological condition in which we can only survive through enormous denial and self-deception. We cannot indefinitely minimize, distort and censor our actual experience when it does not fit our rigid perception of what reality *must* be. This will create an enormous inner conflict, a tension that will surely manifest itself in our relationships.

Unfortunately, when our authoritarian thinking is challenged, many of us simply dig in more stubbornly and deeply. We become preoccupied in our defense. We forget C. S. Lewis's frequent statement: When we say we are defending God, we are often defending ourselves. Insistence on being right leaves us self-absorbed and not open to insight from others. We tell ourselves that if we question even one factor in our thinking, the entire edifice will come tumbling down. This fear of a domino effect will keep us pretending that we remain certain in all our opinions. We may even say that all doubt comes from a rebellious heart and not an inquiring mind. Any intellectual problem, therefore, is a disguised moral problem. And if others disagree with us, regardless of their sincerity, we reduce it to being persecuted for the truth.

Authoritarian thinking insists that order must always take priority over further exploration. While finding a sense of order in our world is important to most of us, anxiety can easily push us toward an excessive demand for mental tidiness. Everything must be figured out and put in its place. All the messy, unexplained facets of life must be shoved into categories. Maintaining the old, secure way of looking at life, even when it doesn't fit our experience, is upheld over admitting uncertainties. The way this comes across in relationships is this: Your experience must fit my preconceptions! If your experience does not seem to match my existing interpretations, then I will twist, minimize or change your experience so that it is compatible with my ideas about the world. Nothing is going to shake the stability or security of my insulated worldview. No matter what your experience seems to be, I will put it in categories manageable for me.

This may be especially tempting when we meet people whose suffering we cannot understand. Rather than recognizing their pain and simply admitting that we don't know why this is happening to them, we frequently offer explanations or platitudes. It becomes very clear after a while that the explanation is a frantic attempt to hold together our own views, rather than to comfort the person in pain. In fact, our explanation for their suffering, as Harold Kushner points out so well, may even be cruel.[2] We may end up blaming the victims, somehow suggesting that the suffering people brought this tragedy on themselves.

Several years ago, I lost my wife in a tragic automobile accident. This same accident nearly took my life as well. As I was recuperating for several months in the hospital, I appreciated the manner in which so many people's hearts reached out to me. Some people very wisely realized that interpretations as to why this had happened were simply not satisfying or adequate. With a loving presence, they embraced my confusion and did not back away from the struggles this raised for my own religious faith.

Others, however, were extremely uncomfortable with the questions this experience provoked. In fact, I could see their own anxiety levels start to rise. Swiftly following this elevation of anxiety was an attempt to quickly offer explanations, *any* explanation, that would restore the security of their thinking. What was abundantly clear was this: their answers were for them, not for me. The fox of doubt had threatened the security of their henhouse. This fox must quickly be eliminated. After all, even unsatisfying answers were better than no answers. This was certainly the conviction of Job's friends. The security of their religious worldview must be protected at all costs. So the primary task was protecting an old way of thinking rather than standing with me in my uncertainty.

It must be stressed that these were often very well-intentioned individuals. They were simply frightened, and this fear led them to cling to religious ideas that minimized or downplayed the problem. They often did not realize that it was their own fear of doubt that they were trying to fix, rather than my particular struggle. My questions and confusions had triggered their own. Unwilling to face and explore the many unsettled mysteries within themselves, how could they possibly hear mine? Also, in our youth, it may be difficult to grasp the deeper struggles, ambiguities and tensions in another's comments. Cheap platitudes are offered, though well intended.

This excessive need for order is why many of us feel forced into seeing a professional counselor or psychotherapist. In effective counseling, we have an opportunity to face our anxiety and insecurity without an immediate need to get rid of them. The therapist is not trying to talk us out of them, tell us they're no big deal or quickly explain them in such a way that they're no longer a problem. In helpful counseling, the focus is on our struggle and not the therapist's need to keep his or her worldview intact.

Prepackaged answers usually sound prescribed. "This was all meant to be," or "You must not question God" are not very helpful comments. They temporarily make life seem manageable, but they ignore the underlying anxiety we all must deal with. They come out of shallow waters and refuse to walk with a person into greater depths. Again, they are not designed to provide comfort. Instead, they are used to eliminate anxiety. Daniel Day Williams addresses this issue:

> The Christian view is never purely Stoic, for the Christian is not ultimately concerned about protecting himself from suffering. In the involvements of love we seek to share life, not immunity from its pain. Identification with the needs of the neighbor is possible only through a willingness to become vulnerable. Jesus was a man of sorrows and acquainted with grief.[3]

If clergy, or anyone else in the people business, claims to have easy, generic answers to human dilemmas, then they need to fully recognize and embrace the particular, concrete dilemmas of people's lives.

While some troubled people may *want* easy answers, precisely because it makes their pain and anxiety seem manageable and meaningful, these platitudes don't last. It's easy to deal in the abstract. But how well do we wade through the crashing waves in another's life, fully acknowledging the level of suffering before we offer hope? It's no problem to sit in our offices and reflect on the human condition, but our quick answers are meaningless unless they can venture into the darkness of another's suffering.

PLURALISM, RADICAL RELATIVISM AND CONVICTION

Having pointed out some of the dangers of authoritarian thinking, it is equally important to say that some perspectives, especially Western religious ones, are often labeled *authoritarian* simply because they dare to speak universally about the human condition. By having the nerve to speak of universals, these groups are said to be authoritarians, exclusivists, intolerant and unaffirming of other perspectives. And worse still, these perspectives are charged with not embracing diversity. The critics quickly move from what Robert Jenson calls the social *reality* of pluralism to the *ideology* of pluralism.[4] Pluralism, as a social reality, simply *is*. We live on a diverse planet with multiple worldviews. This social reality, in and of itself, is neutral. It is a mere description of our context.

However, many individuals want to turn this simple recognition into an ideology, a fundamental philosophy with all sorts of metaphysical assumptions implied. Pluralism becomes elevated into a norm for evaluating all perspectives. All views must not simply be heard and acknowledged; instead, they must be *accepted as legitimate* and *endorsed as right* for the person holding them. Your truth, my truth and everyone else's truth should be held together under a giant canopy of pluralism. Everyone has his or her own epistemological style in this wonderfully diverse situation. Religious, political and ethical perspectives are more like tastes in food or clothing than positions to be compared. In fact, anyone who does not fully embrace the legitimacy of all angles is perceived as intolerant, which once again, is the worst thing that can ever be said about a person. For a Jewish person to actually believe that there is only one God of all people or for a Christian to believe that God's grace is poured out for all in Christ is "narrow-minded, provincial and hopelessly nonpluralistic." Instead, people can only bring their religious views into the arena of pluralism if they embrace the philosophy (religion?) of pluralism itself.

What is painfully missing when pluralism becomes the new gospel is that pluralism, itself, is founded on some definite beliefs, and it makes absolute claims about truth. Saying that "no perspective is universal" is itself a universal statement; saying that there are no metanarratives is itself a metanarrative; claiming the futility of all absolutes is itself an absolute conviction. Ideological pluralism moves from an *is* to an *ought*. Because there *is* an availability of various perspectives, all of them *ought* to be endorsed. But again, when did diversity become sacred? This way of thinking moves from a desire to hear or respect the *people* behind a view to approving that *view*. These are not the same. Yet over and over again, individuals in our culture mistake the differences between accepting a person and endorsing a viewpoint or behavior. Believing that people carry the image of God within them and deserve the opportunity to voice their views does *not* mean we must agree with what they are saying or how they are living. The two are simply not synonymous. Are we to lay down all of our ethical standards simply to be seen as open-minded, accepting people? In order to flexibly embrace every idea or behavior must we denounce all notions of a norm?

The truth of the matter is that no one is a total relativist. We cannot survive without some assumptions about what is good, valuable and even universal. Few of us would say that child molestation may be right for the perpetrator; that stealing someone's valuables simply reveals an alternative set of values; that helping someone in trouble is no different than passing them by. Everything we do each day is predicted by values we hold. And none of us *really* believes those values are completely relative. Whatever we may hear in a classroom, we cannot live that way.

Further, if all perspectives were the same, what would be the point of education? All debate would stop; all conversation would simply be viewed as the revealing of preferences.

Thus, it is important to say this directly: Many of us are very tired of an ideology of pluralism, which hides deeply held philosophical assumptions behind an "innocent" demeanor. The hypocrisy, at times, can nearly be overbearing. Pluralistic ideologues can be as dogmatic in their perspectives as the authoritarians they attack. And attack is precisely what they do. Under the banner of inclusiveness, all are invited except those who do not wave the banner of radical relativism. This view is not simply a threat to ethical principles; it is an assault on the whole idea of intellectual exchange. We end up with a politically correct, bland world in which genuine convictions are forfeited for the mindless endorsement of pluralism. And we need to be aware that when this occurs, *real* dialogue is both impossible and uninteresting.

William G. Perry Jr. of Harvard University conducted an extremely interesting longitudinal study of how college students frequently change their mind.[5] Perry was not interested in the *content* of the students' thinking; instead, he wanted to study any changes in the pattern of their thinking *process*. He was particularly interested in examining how students dealt with the diversity and pluralism at Harvard. He had personally noticed what seemed to be a consistent, sequential pattern of reasoning with the students, and he wanted to further investigate this. Perry's research has been duplicated in other settings and has been well received by the disciplines of psychology and education. Perry essentially found three broad cognitive orientations out of which students think. While students can get stuck at any stage, there is a general developmental progression through these stages.

Perry found that the initial cognitive pattern exhibited by many who began Harvard could best be described as a "dualistic epistemology." In other words, these students approached their classes with a strong expectation to be given the absolute truth about things. The world could be divided between black and white, good and bad, true and false. There were no gray areas. It was the professor's job to provide this absolute truth. At this level there is a demand for complete certainty and a denial that all perspectives involve some degree of risk. There is no need for faith. This mental orientation can be described by what philosophers sometimes call "foundationalism," the belief that we can erect an entire philosophy on the basis of absolutely certain building blocks. Proof must be present.

As students were introduced to a variety of perspectives, many of them recoiled in frustration and wanted simply to know who was right. Some students defensively denied any legitimacy to multiple angles. Eventually, however, most of them went through a kind of epistemological crisis. Perry called this the "crisis of relativism." Students began to realize that there seemed to be some validity to multiple perspectives. For some students, this became a license to think whatever they wanted. If no one knows anyway, then why shouldn't they simply hold their own opinions regardless of the evidence? These students went beyond the recognition that all ideas grow out of a particular context. Instead, all ideas are the *same*. There is no need to look any further because no one will ever know, anyway. All opinions are of equal validity. And some students saw this relativism as more of a reason to despair than to celebrate. They felt overwhelmed and saddened that the search for truth was over.

Yet Perry found that many students went through a further level of development: conviction. As they considered relativism, they could not accept that all ideas were simply of equal value. Some, indeed, were better than others. They were more comprehensive, explained more of the evidence available and were more coherent. They began to realize that while their old demand for absolute certainty could never be realized, they could commit themselves meaningfully to the ideas that made the most sense to them. Students at this stage were willing to acknowledge that *all* views, whether religious or otherwise, began in a kind of faith. It is not necessary to have total proof for commitment to occur. There is a recognized risk here. This faith is not irrational, but it may move beyond what reason can totally settle. In short, it is an Augustinian faith-seeking-understanding model. It begins with assumptions, but then weighs those against evidence available. It recognizes that all perspectives emerge out of social and historical locations, and are therefore finite. However, it does not accept that all perspectives have equal value. Total relativism is a self-contradictory and unlivable philosophy.

Many authoritarians are entrenched in Perry's first mental orientation of a dualistic epistemology. They defend their views with fanaticism, not simply passion. There is enormous anxiety buried beneath their claims of absolute certainty. In order to deny this uncertainty in themselves, they must squash it in others. And as H. Richard Niebuhr reminds us, "self-defense is the most prevalent source of error in all thinking and perhaps especially in theology and ethics."[6] This also applies to many pluralistic ideologues who conceal the "absolute of relativity" beneath their social agenda. As Daniel Taylor puts it, "Even the most ardent pluralist . . . appears tolerant of many different outlooks only because they are *allowed for* in his or her point of view. . . . Most pluralists are not more tolerant of *truly* divergent points of view than those they criticize for intolerance."[7]

NONAUTHORITARIAN CONVERSATION: SOME SUGGESTIONS

All of us will encounter authoritarian thinkers. I would like to suggest a few strategies for dealing with such situations. These suggestions make no claim to *eliminate* all frustration, struggle and reactivity in dealing with judgmentalism. That will not happen. Instead, we can make progress in learning to live underneath our own skin and not allowing authoritarians to control the way we relate to them. This is hard stuff. We will sometimes blow it. Yet our goal, as they say in twelve-step groups, is *progress, not perfection.*

Don't be surprised. We need to remember the manner of authoritarian thinking. We need not be surprised by pulverizing judgments, convenient categories and insulting labels. After all, this is the nature of authoritarian thinking. Rigid, all-or-nothing pronouncements *will* be a part of the authoritarian thought world. We need not be shocked by it. Instead, we can brace ourselves for it. This is reality. It will not help to be appalled, greatly offended or astonished that individuals are capable of this mode of thinking. We do not live in a world free of judgmentalism. While we may not like it, we need to recognize it as a part of life.

It is easy to forget this inevitable encounter with authoritarian thinking. We may walk around with an image in our minds of how healthy people *should* relate to each other. We may unconsciously expect that everyone else has this same view of interpersonal relationships. And when we run into authoritarian thinking, we may recoil with astonishment. If we let ourselves, we can ruminate over the encounter for the rest of the day. "They have no right to be that way!" we may say. We may become shocked and preoccupied. Our day, if we're not careful, can be ruined by the unfortunate experience of bumping into this type of thinking. Yet the authoritarian thinking is not causing us nearly as much trouble as (a) our shock and outrage that there are people like this and (b) a belief that we have a right to never have to deal with one of them! We bring unnecessary stress on ourselves as we can't seem to let go of our outrage that there are people like this in the world.

Encounter different perspectives. Whenever we can, it's helpful to encourage authoritarian thinkers into a situation in which they confront different viewpoints. When individuals have to face well-intentioned people of alternative perspectives, they may begin to loosen their convictions that they *own* the truth. When they rub shoulders with a well-intentioned person of an opposing viewpoint, it is not so easy to write them off without some discomfort.

Take on other perspectives. Invite black-or-white thinkers to take on the perspective of others. We can ask authoritarian thinkers how other people may have arrived at their point of view. If authoritarians start to see the context of other people's lives and thoughts, they may begin to recognize that their own thinking, also, emerges in a particular context and is limited. As we have already seen, authoritarians are weak on perspective-taking skills. They need practice in placing themselves in another's frame of reference. Perhaps they will begin to see that all thought, even ideas about ultimate matters, occurs in a specific and limited location. Indeed, we all see through a glass darkly.

Questions such as the following may be helpful in breaking through the authoritarian's judgment of another: "What do you think this other person was feeling and experiencing when she did that?" or "How might this other person have developed those ideas you believe are so strange?" or "If you had walked in his shoes, what do you think you would be struggling with?" These questions are designed to get authoritarians into the worlds of other people. Once they do this, their judgments of these people will not come so easily.

Understanding their fear. When dealing with authoritarian thinkers, it is sometimes helpful to remember that they may be abusive because they are so anxious. We need to look for the insecurity beneath what seems like a swollen ego. Fear often drives the bus of aggression. A craving for security can be similar to an addiction. In fact, absolute certainty can function like a drug of choice. Authoritarians often believe that even a small cog in their grand conceptual scheme will ruin everything. Consequently, they become hostile when questioned. They do not want to rethink their world. Probably none of us delights in the loss of security that accompanies a challenge to our belief system. But for authoritarians, the challenge is unbearable. Therefore, fighting overthrows discussing; conquering overshadows sharing; and winning means more than searching. Perhaps it's helpful to silently ask ourselves in the presence of an authoritarian thinker: "What are you afraid of?" Focusing on this underlying fear may help us be more compassionate.

Recognizing their doubt. We also need to remind ourselves that when authoritarians react to our uncertainty, this reaction is probably based on a denial of their own uncertainty. Our doubts may be their doubts. In fact, this may be what authoritarian thinking is fighting—the uncertainty within itself. Unable to admit this, it externalizes the doubt and attacks it in others. What we cannot accept within ourselves we project on anyone who raises disturbing questions.

Confronting our preunderstanding. We need to realize that everyone comes from somewhere. In other words, we need to fully grasp that our perspectives are always shaped by the unique cluster of influences that are part of our past. We bring a history to each conversation. That history has obviously influenced our angle on life. Our angles are indeed different. And there is no such thing as an angleless perspective, no such thing as someone who comes from nowhere, no one who has a completely neutral mind. To have lived is to have been influenced by factors that are unique to each of us. We are not just objective calculators; we are *involved* in life. We cannot have lived and developed without forming what is often called "preunderstanding" or a unique perspective we bring to each conversation. We don't start from scratch when we engage people. In fact, without a guiding framework from our past, we would not even be able to understand anyone's experience.

Authoritarian thinkers often claim that they speak from a completely objective and neutral place, a no-spin zone. This is simply impossible. We are all creatures of a particular time, place and language. We need not apologize for this social and historical limitation, but neither should we ignore it and act as if we are speaking from a completely detached, objective place. We don't have timeless, spaceless opinions. While we can distance ourselves from some of our assumptions, we'll never succeed in completely removing them. They will creep back in and inform us in ways we don't realize.

I mention this because I often hear people say, "I call it the way it is!" While I appreciate their honesty, they seem to have no realization that their mind, like everyone else's, interprets the world through their own mental filter. This filter is unique to them and is not everyone else's filter. Again, we all carry baggage when we enter a conversation. Judgmentalism always forgets this and reacts to others because they do not come from *our* world of our taken-for-granted assumptions. Yet, no one has a complete lock on absolute truth all the time, so we should be humbly open to listening to other people's opinions and perspectives. While we can form convictions based on our own experience and available information, we should remain open to new ways of thinking.

Validate others' experiences. We need to move away from the notion that "if we haven't experienced it, it must not be real." This attitude elevates our own experience, which is always limited, to the state of a final standard for *all* experience. It is helpful to regularly remind ourselves that other people have had experiences of which we know nothing. Again, while our experiences provide us with a framework, they are not the final frame of reference for everyone. We can use our experiences to advance understanding; however, we can overextend it to advance misunderstanding.

Sometimes I have had no idea of what someone was talking about, only to find out later, after my own experience had been expanded, exactly what they meant. I did not understand back then, but I certainly do now. Back then, I thought they were strange; now I understand. Most of us have had this experience.

Focus on the true goal of conversation. While argument may emerge in a conversation, it should never occur simply for its own sake. The argument needs to be enveloped in a deeper commitment to truth and mutual respect. Stated differently, increasing our understanding needs to overshadow winning a debate! The joy of chasing a topic does not need to be weighted down with a preoccupation with who's winning. Scorekeeping is unnecessary. This is not easy because most of us are very invested in our basic convictions. Yet when we drop the necessity to outmaneuver our "opponent" and concentrate instead on gaining insight with our conversational partner, then real advances can occur.

Perhaps nothing comes easier than to treat an authoritarian in an authoritarian manner. But again, the ultimate goal of life is not to crack their façade and reveal how insecure authoritarian thinkers really are. The point is not to treat the authoritarian like a cognitive leper. The goal is instead to invite greater humanness in a dialogue enveloped by care. We can affirm the person while disagreeing with the viewpoint. Uncaring argument does not help in the pursuit of truth.

7

"Grace-Full" Living with a Clear Mind and a Generous Heart

Thus far, I have focused on some ways to become less judgmental toward ourselves and others. I have tried to suggest a few things that can help promote and sustain self-acceptance. However, I've been direct about a deeply held belief: I do not think that any of us has the power to completely accept ourselves in isolation. Once the suspicion of inadequacy has set in, I cannot pull myself up by my psychological bootstraps and declare myself acceptable. The dark forces of rejection are too powerful. I may *act* like I've conquered the acceptance problem, but down deep, I will crave an acceptance that must come from a transcendent Source. How does it help to "declare myself okay" when it is my own testimony that is on trial in the first place? Again, I may relentlessly attempt to achieve self-acceptance on my own. I may even want to stay disconnected from people while I make this effort. But all individual healing begins in the context of an accepting relationship. Without this help, I cannot get out from under my own sense of condemnation.

A Community of Grace
This inability to save ourselves psychologically is simply part of our

limits as human beings. We may rebel against our own finitude and say we need no one. But we cannot muscle up the individual strength to pull ourselves out of a sense of inadequacy. There are no successful fix-it-at-home kits. It simply won't work alone. We cannot give ourselves what we do not have. Self-judgment is too strong. Yet in spite of our own inadequate efforts, Divine acceptance is available. Daniel Day Williams describes this experience:

> This power is grace. It does not come in the first instance as a summons to take heart, and to gird up our moral wills, but rather as an invitation to confess our inability to release ourselves from bondage, a call to open ourselves to a love which is freely given, which has never let us go, and which is ours on the sole condition that we are willing to trust the God who so loves us.[1]

Our task is not to do things frantically in order to feel that we have earned and deserved this grace. Instead, we need to stand still, take it in, celebrate this new reality and allow it to motivate us toward a life of gratitude.

The abstract notion of acceptability, however, may not be very plausible to us unless it is concretely embodied. Vague notions of our acceptance are not transforming. Joseph Cooke puts this point beautifully:

> If we happen to be in a situation where no single living person really knows us, or loves us just as we are, or reaches out to give of himself to meet our needs, it is almost impossible to find very much meaning in the idea of God's acceptance. The grace is all theoretical—off in the fantasy world of wish fulfillment or empty intellectualization. But the legalism, the non-grace, the sense of worthlessness and rejection are real. They are what we

experience and live with every day. It's hard to rest in God's uncondemning love and acceptance if we feel that the people around us are ignoring us, condemning us, criticizing us, putting us down. If grace is to mean anything to us, it has to have feet that run to meet us, hands that reach out to us, eyes that see us, a mouth that speaks to us, a heart that loves us and cares what happens to us.[2]

Our self-judgment feeds off criticism and negativity from people around us. It knows that a cynical, judgmental attitude is like a virus entering our bodies. Out of fear, we use other people's unfavorable comments about us as ammunition for self-attack. Other judgmental people provide our own self-judgment with bigger clubs to beat us with.

It is therefore crucial to surround ourselves with a community of grace. This connection will help build us up. We can often be accepted into accepting ourselves. In other words, as we risk being known, and find ourselves acceptable to others, it becomes more feasible to also accept ourselves. This community is crucial in providing us with insulation against judgmentalism. We need to see a piece of our acceptability in a friend's smile; learn to trust ourselves as we are treated with dignity; and recognize our own value as we are offered a compassionate respect. A church enveloped by grace can help us look at ourselves without a fear of ultimate rejection. As William Hordern reminds us, "Jesus says, 'If you love me, you will keep my commandments' (John 14:15). The law, by contrast, always says: If you will keep my commandments, I will love you."[3] God's grace provides the deep assurance that we can look at even our ugliest inclination and know that we still stand accepted. We need to know ahead of time that it's going to be okay. We can be free to both explore and confess our shortcomings without the voice of radical condemnation hovering above us: we can risk and find out what we're about. We must have this deep assurance that we are acceptable no matter what we dig up. Compassion and love pull back the curtain of secrecy. Grace is necessary for us to understand deeply who we are. Grace embraces our entire being as it offers healing forgiveness and the motivation for change, and then it encourages us to love fully. We need not remain obsessed with our own faults. Instead, we can respond to divine acceptance with a joyful appreciation and deep gratitude.

This is especially important because many of us live with anticipations of judgment. Previous experiences of being ridiculed, exposed or shamed have set us up to be leery. We shy away from where we're not welcome, and we withhold our secrets when we smell rejection. God's grace, on the other hand, opens the door to self-discovery. And when we truly experience acceptance, we usually want to give it away to others. Acceptance is the birthplace of compassion and gratitude. Grace provides a desire to give back to life what we have been given.

A community of grace helps provide a healthy vision of growth and spiritual development. Judgmental thinking, on the other hand, *feeds* off what others are doing wrong. When our judgmental tendencies are the most active, it is normally because our minds are inactive, bored and uninterested in our own spiritual and emotional growth. To fill this void, we become preoccupied with others. Blasting away at them becomes the hobby that takes away our boredom. After all, it is an easy, relatively effortless conversation.

A community of grace promotes positive activities and thoughts rather than opportunities to judge. At a workshop I once attended, I remember hearing Wayne Muller, a minister and psychotherapist, talk about how a stampeding elephant can nearly tear up a village *until* he is given something to hold onto with his long trunk.[4] Similarly, he said, our minds need something hopeful and positive to hold. Otherwise, we can be quite capable of negative, even destructive, thinking. When our minds are not seeking truth, beauty, goodness and other healthy things, we are often vulnerable to a takeover of judgmental, poisonous thinking.

Another way of putting this is simply that a positive mind does not have the time or energy to waste on useless judgmentalism. It is too busy following a healthy path to constantly criticize the world around itself. A desire for expansion, growth and improvement is much more important. Our ambition prevents us from a need to put down others.

A community of grace also helps us maintain a healthy awareness of our own struggles and shortcomings. This is not a debilitating, shaming awareness of our own dark side but a keen perception of our human limitations. We see a clear link with other people's weaknesses because we are quite aware of our own. Others' mistakes don't seem so foreign or unusual to us. A great deal of our judgmental reactions to others is based on failure to look at ourselves. Unaware of our own issues, we attempt to defeat our anxiety by attacking these same problems in others. As we become more aware and accepting of our own faults, we have less need to assault others.

A community of grace allows us to borrow its vision and hope when our own seems to be faltering. As Daniel Taylor puts it:

> Sometimes life's troubles may so overwhelm me that I cannot for a time sustain a belief in God's loving concern for me and my fellow creatures. In my humanity, I may, like many of my biblical predecessors in faith, despair or even rage against God. At that point you must believe for me. Do not insist that I still believe. Do not whip the mule that has collapsed under the bur-

den. Do what you can to lighten the burden and wait patiently until I have regained my strength. And someday I will do the same for you.[5]

A community of grace supports and nurtures us during our dark nights of the soul. It does not run away from our heartbrokenness, our anger or our depletion of hope. It invites only our honesty and is not threatened by our doubts. It does not try to talk us out of our crises; instead, it supports us through them.

A community of grace deliberately practices empathy. The ability to understand the feelings of another is a skill we can learn and develop. Many of us may think of empathy as requiring us to feel the exact feelings someone else feels. In some cases, however, that might block the process of empathy. The key is *understanding* others' feelings rather than *feeling them yourself*. That understanding may, of course, trigger some of our own feelings, but the point is that this is primarily a mental practice, a thought exercise. We place ourselves in others' shoes and take on their perspective. As we have already noted, this does not mean that we always agree with them. But we can make enormous progress in seeing why others think and feel the way they do.

This point needs to be heavily stressed because a lot of us may think that we are not very emotional people, and hence, not very good at empathizing with anyone. We may even think that empathy is simply a skill some are born with and others are not. The fact is, however, that empathy can be learned and taught. We may not feel like a natural in the empathy business, but we *can* make definite progress in improving our ability to take on another's perspective.

It helps when we daily commit ourselves to understanding *people* before criticizing *behavior*. We need to remind ourselves that all behavior occurs in a context, and if we have no knowledge of the context, it's probably wise to withhold judgment. We need to remember how much we dislike being judged by someone who doesn't know *our* situation. Here is a perfect opportunity to treat others as we wish to be treated. This is an opportunity to recognize our common humanity with others and not pretend that their wrongful actions are totally foreign to us. I especially appreciate the words of Bill W. of Alcoholics Anonymous:

Finally, we begin to see that all people, including ourselves, are to some extent emotionally ill as well as frequently wrong, and then we approach true tolerance and see what real love for our fellows actually means. It will become more and more evident as we go forward that it is pointless to become angry, or to get hurt by people who, like us, are suffering from the pains of growing up.[6]

Empathy pushes us to recognize our common humanity with others rather than our "entitlement" to judge them.

Empathy also helps ease others by creating a space for them to be themselves. Most of us can quickly name the people to whom we would want to talk if something were troubling us. Almost without exception, a trait of that person is being relaxed and nonjudgmental, someone we're comfortable to be around. We can breathe easily around this person. We can allow our thoughts and feelings to unfold. We don't have to censor ourselves. In short, we feel unthreatened enough to explore what is bothering us.

A community of grace offers hospitality, a word beautifully developed by Henri Nouwen. Consider his eloquent description:

Hospitality, therefore, means primarily the creation of a free space where the stranger can enter and become a friend instead of an enemy. Hospitality is not to change people, but to offer them space where change can take place. It is not to bring men and women over to our side, but to offer freedom not disturbed by dividing lines. It is not to lead our neighbor into a corner where there are no alternatives left, but to open a wide spectrum of options for choice and commitment. . . . The paradox of hospitality is that it wants to create emptiness, not a fearful emptiness, but a friendly emptiness where strangers can enter and discover themselves as created free; free to sing their own songs, speak their own languages, dance their own dances; free also to leave and follow their own vocations. Hospitality is not a subtle invitation to adopt the lifestyle of the host, but the gift of a chance for the guest to find his own.[7]

Hospitality is thus a noninvasive invitation for others to be themselves. It promotes freedom and self-acceptance.

CONVICTION, CARE AND SPEAKING UP

Being kind, courteous and empathic in our relationships does *not* mean that we cannot have definite convictions. In fact, everyone holds convictions about something. Everyone also has faith in something. And everyone is invested in something. Christians need not apologize for their allegiance to the gospel. Instead, they should celebrate it as the foundational pillar of their hope. There is no contradiction between being warmhearted and firm in our convictions, especially when we believe that God's love is the most basic reality of life. While Paul encourages us to "speak the truth *in love*," he *does* say to speak the truth. A conflict-avoidant strategy that unassertively seeks peace at all costs will not be helpful. This hope of a world without disagreement and conflict is a hope we need to let die. David Augsburger puts this well:

> The hope for peace can be turned into a dream of escaping all tensions, avoiding stress, evading anxiety. The hope for togetherness can become a wish for no differences, no conflict, no diversity. The hope for acceptance can grow into a demand that there be no criticism, no negatives, no confrontation. The hope for harmony can emerge as an attempt at feeling no anger, no arousal, no hostile feelings. The hope for love can be distorted into a need to control, manipulate, dominate. The hope for adequacy can be expressed as a belief that tender, sad, or painful feelings must be suppressed or denied.[8]

Many arenas of conversation are, quite frankly, unfriendly. A conflict-avoidant attempt to understand how "we're all really saying the same thing" simply will not be effective. While we can be tactful, caring and open to others, Christian convictions, no matter how healthily stated, will offend some. As long as they are kept in the closet and treated as a private spiritual hobby, there may be no problems, but the minute these convictions are thought to seriously influence our view of life, there is trouble. And unfortunately, the problem is compounded by some who present the Christian message in a belligerent, self-righteous, know-it-all manner. Christians who care about a clear mind should be appalled at the way Christianity is often represented on our television screens. Is it any wonder that the general public sometimes thinks that Christianity is intellectually indefensible? I salute Christian scholars, such as Mark Noll, who indict many Christians for not loving God with their minds.[9] The damage done to Christian witness because of many media figures is a sad reality. So we need to be prepared to deal with caricatures and distorted images of Christianity rather than assume that people in the public arena know what authentic Christianity is all about.

We should also remind ourselves that the message of grace will not be very meaningful to individuals who find nothing wrong with their lives, who have built up these judgmental defenses as a way to avoid anxiety and pain. As William Hordern reminds us, "The forgiveness of sins could not be good news to someone who was not aware of any need to be forgiven."[10] Or, as Don Browning puts it:

> We cannot understand the meaning of forgiveness unless we first throw ourselves into a radical concern about the nature of right moral action. We cannot be delivered from the curse of the law unless first of all we know, contemplate, and strive to keep the law.[11]

We are not in the business of cheap grace. Without some sense of defeat, the message of acceptance will mean little. While some of us may become more dramatically shipwrecked than others, we are all desperate. This reality hasn't changed since Paul's own experience with those who sought to take advantage of grace or felt that they were automatically entitled to it (Romans 5:20; 6:1-2).

An authentic Christian voice must offer both a caring and prophetic side. It must support, encourage and accept. And it must also challenge, confront and invite. It must nurture people and challenge injustice. It must keep an eye on people's God-given potential while it fully acknowledges where people *currently* are on their journeys. It must look beneath arrogant displays and see the frightened, insecure people beneath the grandiosity, but it must also invite people back to their own vulnerability and ultimate dependence on God. It must challenge and dismantle idolatry while holding a safety net of grace beneath others when they fall. It must not enable others to live irresponsibly under a shallow view of grace that permits everything. Instead, it must convey grace as *both* radical acceptance and a motivator for change. It must not back down from pointing out things that are ultimately destructive for both individual and social life.

An authentic Christian voice refuses "bystander apathy" while it watches the world continue to deteriorate. And though it does not consider its job to police people's moral lives, it is unafraid to speak up about significant ethical matters. It will not allow fear of appearing dogmatic to keep it silent, while a choir of "tolerant" perspectives peddle their own dogmas. It will freely admit that its perspective begins in faith but also point out that everyone else's view also begins with faith in something. It will use reason as a means of better understanding its faith. It will attempt to be fair and respectful in public discourse. However, it will reject the idea that while a Judeo-Christian view is biased, secular views speak with "total objectivity." It will fully acknowledge the damage done under a distorted image of the gospel, but it will *also* point out what Christianity has contributed to the Western world, refusing to join the bandwagon of religion bashing. And while it will say that some unfortunate expressions of Christianity have been psychologically damaging, it will proclaim the resources within the Christian tradition that can lead to a very fulfilling life.

Our current cultural situation offers us a great opportunity to speak the truth in love and quit engaging in mudslinging, judgmental language. James Davison Hunter vividly describes the polarizing animosity in much of contemporary debate:

> The rhetoric infused into public discourse by each side is so similar that without identifying the object of derision and aversion, it is nearly impossible to distinguish which of the two coalitions is speaking. In each case the rhetoric is divisive and

inflammatory. But what makes contemporary public discourse even more inflammatory is the appeal to sensationalism. Is it really true, as some progressivist voices claim, that "religious fervor now combines with reactionary politics resulting in a neo-fascism that threatens the foundations of American life? Or that 'the result of a political takeover by the religious right' might bring into existence a kind of Christian Nazism (with the Bible as *Mein Kampf*) whose manipulated multitudes goosestep mercilessly over the godless"? Is it really true, as some orthodox voices have claimed, that "those of the humanistic stripe want to see all Bibles banned in America . . . to see all church doors closed"? Or that if nonbelieving politicians are elected it would be necessary to "put your Bible under your mattress, fold up your American flags and throw away all your coins that say 'In God We Trust' "? But sensationalism and exaggeration, regardless of the party and the object of disfavor, always foster fear, mistrust, and resentment. . . . In the end such language may titillate even the most dispassionate of listeners, but it can only lead to one conclusion: the further polarization of public discourse.[12]

It is way past time to throw down our stones. Conviction does not have to involve belligerence.

Furthering the reactionary, uncaring verbal war games will not help anyone. Inflammatory language will prevent others from hearing our message. There is dignity and strength in remaining responsive rather than reactionary. Further, we need not think that it is completely up to us to bring people into the reality of truth. That grandiose view of apologetics only makes us self-preoccupied, nervous and inauthentic in our relationships with others. We are called to witness to the truth, not force people to see it. We can control no one; nor should we want to. Most people know when they are being manipulated, and manipulation has no place in sharing God's good news.

CONCLUSION

Eliminating all of our judgmentalism is a nice thought but not a likely reality. Snap judgments, impatient criticisms and unfair condemnations will indeed continue to enter our thinking. We can make enormous progress in understanding and detoxifying them. We can cultivate an attitude of acceptance (of ourselves and others) as a daily spiritual practice. To mirror God's love in our own lives, we need to see that love mirrored in those around us. And there is no greater honor in this world than to reflect the grace that has been given to us. We will occasionally relapse into old patterns of unfriendly put-downs. But when we *do* become judgmental, we can catch ourselves sooner and intervene. We didn't become judgmental overnight, so it may take a while to change this pattern. But the wait will be an active one, full of the promise of a new way of relating to others.

One of the most difficult journeys in life is the road from hostility to compassion. Compassion is not something we can simply dredge up in a strong-willed, Pelagian manner. As Augsburger puts it:

Compassion is not something we create, not something we can force from our soul, not something we just *do*. Compassion is something we *discover:* We discover it when we realize, with some painful objectivity, that we are not totally unlike those who have hurt us, that we are more than a little similar, that the other's evil action is mirrored in my answering evil impulse—justified as it may be—and the good that is in my longing for justice may, in some way, be present in the offender too.[13]

Yet while compassion is ultimately a gift of grace, it is also something we can further cultivate and practice in our lives. In short, it is a spiritual discipline.

Throughout this book, I have tried to offer specific suggestions for decreasing judgmentalism and enhancing our sense of God's acceptance. It takes courage to drop our guard and look squarely at our own defensive postures and unhealthy interpersonal patterns. This self-inventory necessitates assurance, in advance, that we are accepted no matter what we find within ourselves, and God's (and other people's) acceptance allows greater self-discovery. This self-discovery, when enveloped by a motivating grace, helps us become less judgmental and more caring toward others. My hope is that this book aids that process of self-understanding, less judging, greater accepting, solid conviction and deeper conversation.

NOTES

Chapter 1: I'm Judgmental, You're Judgmental
[1]James Davison Hunter, *Culture Wars: The Struggle to Define America* (New York: Basic Books, 1991), pp. 135-58.
[2]Roberta Bondi, *To Love as God Loves* (Minneapolis: Fortress, 1987), p. 35.

Chapter 2: Making Judgments Without Being Judgmental
[1]Henri Nouwen, *The Wounded Healer* (New York: Doubleday, 1972), p. 72.
[2]Daniel Taylor, *The Myth of Certainty: The Reflective Christian and the Risk of Commitment* (Downers Grove, Ill.: InterVarsity Press, 1992), p. 18.

Chapter 3: Insecure Arrogance vs. Confident Humility
[1]Henri Nouwen, *The Wounded Healer* (New York: Doubleday, 1972), p. 63.
[2]Carl Rogers, *On Becoming a Person* (Boston: Houghton Mifflin, 1961), pp. 18-19.
[3]Terry D. Cooper, *Sin, Pride & Self-Acceptance: The Problem of Identity in Theology & Psychology* (Downers Grove, Ill.: InterVarsity Press, 2003).
[4]David G. Myers, *The Inflated Self* (New York: Seabury Press, 1980).
[5]David G. Myers, *Psychology Through the Eyes of Faith* (San Francisco: Harper and Row, 1987), especially chapter 21, pp. 129-36.
[6]Myers, *The Inflated Self*, p. 21.
[7]Ibid., p. 24.
[8]Karen Horney, *Neurosis and Human Growth* (New York: W. W. Norton, 1950).
[9]Christopher Lasch, *The Culture of Narcissism* (New York: W. W. Norton, 1979).
[10]Some of these include Edwin Schur, *The Awareness Trap: Self-Absorption Instead of Social Change* (New York: McGraw-Hill, 1976); Martin Gross, *The Psychological Society* (New York: Simon and Schuster, 1978); Paul Vitz, *Psychology as Religion: The Cult of Self-Worship*, 2nd ed. (Grand Rapids: Eerdmans, 1994); and David Myers, *The Inflated Self*, which I have already mentioned.
[11]Donald Capps, *The Depleted Self: Sin in a Narcissistic Age* (Minneapolis: Fortress, 1993), p. 4.

[12]Søren Kierkegaard, *The Concept of Anxiety*, trans. Reidar Thomte (Princeton, N.J.: Princeton University Press, 1980).

[13]Before reading some of the much more difficult works of Kohut, a very good place to begin is *Heinz Kohut: The Chicago Institute Lectures*, ed. Paul Tolpin and Marian Tolpin (Hillsdale, N.J.: The Analytic Press, 1996).

[14]For an excellent study of Kohut's life, see Charles B. Strozier, *Heinz Kohut: The Making of a Psychoanalyst* (New York: Other Press, 2001).

[15]David W. Augsburger, *Helping People Forgive* (Louisville: Westminster John Knox Press, 1996), p. 75.

[16]Ibid., p. 76.

[17]Ibid., p. 79.

[18]Kohut, *Chicago Institute Lectures*, pp. 243-74.

[19]Alan Loy McGinnis, *Confidence: How to Succeed at Being Yourself* (Minneapolis: Augsburg, 1987), p. 21.

[20]Fredrick Buechner, *Wishful Thinking: A Theological ABC* (New York: HarperCollins, 1973), p. 95.

Chapter 4: Responding with Judgments vs. Reacting with Judgmentalism

[1]Aaron Beck, *Prisoners of Hate: The Cognitive Basis of Anger, Hostility, and Violence* (New York: HarperCollins, 1999).

[2]David W. Augsburger, *Anger and Assertiveness in Pastoral Care* (Minneapolis: Fortress, 1979), p. 22.

[3]David Augsburger, *Caring Enough to Confront* (Scottsdale, Penn: Herald Press, 1973), p. 11.

[4]Ibid., pp. 52-53.

Chapter 5: Guilty Judgments vs. Shameful Judgmentalism

[1]Dietrich Bonhoeffer, *Life Together* (New York: Harper and Row, 1954), p. 112.

[2]Thomas C. Oden, *The Structure of Awareness* (Nashville: Abingdon, 1969), pp. 23-45.

[3]Thomas C. Oden, *Guilt Free* (Nashville: Abingdon, 1980), pp. 34-35.

[4]Ibid., pp. 46-51.

[5]Karen Horney, *Our Internal Conflicts: A Constructive Theory of Neurosis* (New York: W. W. Norton, 1955).

[6]C. S. Lewis, *The Four Loves* (New York: Harcourt Brace Jovanovich, 1991), p. 112.

[7]Reinhold Niebuhr, *The Nature and Destiny of Man*, vol. 1 (New York: Scribner, 1964), p. 271.

[8]Oden, *Structure of Awareness*, p. 258.

Chapter 6: Authoritative Judgments vs. Authoritarian Judgmentalism

[1]Howard J. Clinebell Jr., *The Mental Health Ministry of the Local Church* (Nashville: Abingdon, 1972), p. 34.

[2]Harold Kushner, *When Bad Things Happen to Good People* (New York: Avon, 1981).

[3]Daniel Day Williams, *The Minister and the Care of Souls* (New York: Harper and Row, 1961), p. 24.

[4]Robert W. Jenson, "The God-Wars," in *Either/Or: The Gospel or Neopaganism*, ed. Carl E. Braaten and Robert W. Jenson (Grand Rapids: Eerdmans, 1995), pp. 23-36.

[5]William G. Perry Jr., *Forms of Intellectual and Ethical Behavior in the College Years* (New York: Holt, Rinehart and Winston, 1970).

[6]H. Richard Niebuhr, *The Meaning of Revelation* (New York: Macmillan, 1941), p. x.

[7]Daniel Taylor, *The Myth of Certainty: The Reflective Christian and the Risk of Commitment* (Downers Grove, Ill.: InterVarsity Press, 1992), p. 24.

Chapter 7: "Grace-Full" Living with a Clear Mind and a Generous Heart

[1]Daniel Day Williams, *The Minister and the Care of Souls* (New York: Harper and Row, 1961), p. 75.

[2]Joseph Cooke, *Free for the Taking* (Old Tappan, N.J.: Fleming H. Revell, 1975), p. 184.

[3]William Hordern, *Living By Grace* (Philadelphia: Westminster Press, 1975), p. 136.

[4]See Wayne Muller, *Legacy of the Heart: The Spiritual Advantages of a Painful Childhood* (New York: Simon and Schuster, 1992).

[5]Daniel Taylor, *The Myth of Certainty: The Reflective Christian and the Risk of Commitment* (Downers Grove, Ill.: InterVarsity Press, 1992), p. 110.

[6]Alcoholics Anonymous, *Twelve Steps and Twelve Traditions* (New York: A.A. World Services, 1952), p. 92.

[7]Henri Nouwen, *Reaching Out* (Garden City, N.Y.: Image, 1986), pp. 71-72.

[8]David Augsburger, *When Enough Is Enough* (Ventura, Calif.: Regal, 1984), p. 105.

[9]Mark A. Noll, *The Scandal of the Evangelical Mind* (Grand Rapids: Eerdmans, 1994).

[10]William Hordern, *Living By Grace* (Philadelphia: Westminster Press, 1975), p. 113.

[11]Don S. Browning, *The Moral Context of Pastoral Care* (Philadelphia: Westminster Press, 1976), p. 125.

[12]James Davison Hunter, *Culture Wars: The Struggle to Define America* (New York: Basic Books, 1991), pp. 152-53.

[13]David Augsburger, *Hate-Work: Working Through the Pain and Pleasures of Hate* (Louisville, Ky.: Westminster John Knox Press, 2004), p. 50.

Name Index